GOLDEN DAYS

Black Hackle.
Coch-y-bondhu.
Dark Red Quill

Red Palmer.
Tupps' Indispensable
Governor with yellow tag.

Flat winged Alder.
Red Quill
Blue Upright

Watercolour by Romilly Fedden

Photograph by Yacine M'Seffar   www.yacinephoto.com

GOLDEN DAYS

FROM THE FISHING-LOG OF
A PAINTER IN BRITTANY

BY

ROMILLY FEDDEN

Coch-y-Bonddu Books
2012

Golden Days:
From the Fishing-Log of a Painter in Brittany
by
Romilly Fedden

This book was first published in 1919 by A. & C. Black,
with a second edition by the same publisher in 1949.
This edition published by Coch-y-Bonddu Books in 2012.

New introductory material
© 2011 Claude Belloir, Geoffrey Bucknall, Nick Lyons.

© 2011 Coch-y-Bonddu Books Ltd, Machynlleth, Powys SY20 8DG
01654 702837

www.ffcl.com   www.anglebooks.com

ISBN 978-1-904784-37-1

A MA FEMME,

Pour qu'elle se rapelle Rosebraz,
les sabots bretons, la vieille jupe de gros drap,
et maint petit sentier à travers les landes
que nous avons parcourus ensemble.

CONTENTS

INTRODUCTION TO 1949 EDITION

I read Romilly Fedden's *Golden Days* as soon as it was published in 1919. It has been my constant companion ever since. I was not long back from Russia, where during the First World War I had spent four and a half strenuous years including a term of imprisonment under the Bolsheviks. I had come home, disillusioned by war and revolution and dispirited by my own failure. I wanted solitude and spiritual comfort. From boyhood I had been a passionate angler and, like most fishermen, a regular buyer of books on fishing. There were and still are mainly expert treatises or else reminiscences of personal achievement by the riverside and, in the main, their appeal is limited to anglers. Then I found *Golden Days*. Here was something entirely different from the ordinary book on fishing. True it is that fishing is the web on which this exquisite story is spun, but from the delicate descriptions of nature I knew instinctively that the author must be not only an artist in paint and words but also a man of exceptional personality and compelling charm. I found it difficult to place the book in its proper category. I know that I felt and still feel that I am a better man for the reading of it. Of one thing I was certain: *Golden Days* was a book that would attract the ordinary reader as much as the angler. Two or three years later John Buchan was to give me the definition I required. 'The enduring book on fishing', he wrote, 'must be the revelation of the inner heart of nature or of a man's own soul.' With the substitution of 'and' for 'or' in the quotation, *Golden Days* is such a book.

My enthusiasm sent me in search of the author, but he had left England and, as I had to go abroad again, I never met him. During the recent war, when I could read nothing but old favourites, I renewed my search. Romilly Fedden was dead. For a time my war work drew me close to Professor E. L. Woodward who, I discovered to my joy, had known Fedden well. Then, again quite by accident, I met the son, and in this way I have been able to make my own picture of the man.

Romilly Fedden, the son of a man who painted and himself a painter by profession, was forty when the First World War started. He joined up at once. Professor Woodward, who was with him during their period of training in England, describes him as gentle and full of pleasant irony. He hated soldiering, but never complained. Nor was he at all a bad soldier – even though his commanding officer, a dug-out and a former prison governor, could make nothing of him. One day he said to Fedden in front of everyone in the mess: 'I hear you are an artist. Would you mind painting our big drum?' Fedden, six foot three in height and broad in proportion, said not a word, but, by painting the drum with care and delicacy and adding touches of heraldry and regimental exploits, gave great pleasure to his C.O. Gentleness was the chief characteristic of this giant figure of a man who, because he hated war, regarded it as a duty to be borne without complaining. On another occasion Woodward and he sat together while their brigade had to listen to a long lecture on discipline from a very high general straight from the War Office. As they came away, Fedden, who had a pleasant voice with a slight stammer, said to Woodward: 'D-d-d-discipline – d-d-d-discipline is the o-o-one thing I hate.'

By all accounts he had great presence, good looks and a most attractive personality. All who knew him speak of his exceptional charm. Professor Woodward who, I think, sums him up best wrote to me recently: 'he made me feel that the civilised world had not wholly disappeared and that I need not mind the follies and catastrophes of mankind. In 1915 we planned, after the war, to buy a disused watermill and make our living out of it ... It seems a long time ago, and people didn't grow up like Fedden in the years between 1919 and 1939.'

Romilly Fedden came out of the war a convinced pacifist. In this sense he was a war casualty. He almost ceased to paint; for a time he refused even to fish. Partly because of his post-war attitude, but mainly I imagine from inclination, he withdrew to France where in odd provincial towns his figure must have been a familiar sight as he hung over a bridge and watched the river. It is significant of the man that, although a painter of distinction, the running water always commanded his first attention. *Golden Days* was perhaps the last time that he really expressed himself.

The book itself has the modest sub-title of *From the Fishing-Log of a Painter in Brittany*. There is much about fishing in the book, and attractive fishing at that, for Fedden has the art of making you see with your own eyes not only the river but also the whole scene in which it is set. As a writer he has that rarest of virtues – a faculty of vision which is both individual and sympathetic. At the riverside he was an unorthodox and thoughtful fisher, and many of his comments will interest the lover of nature as much as the angler. He is, too, a painter of character. All his Breton friends become your friends, and in Jean Pierre, who 'was wise in the ways of all creatures which move beneath the water' and who, like Fedden himself, hated all governments, he has drawn a superb portrait of a Breton self-taught fisher. There are, too, many pleasant pictures of the Breton life that he loved so well. Lastly there are his reflections on life and on the modern civilisation that he hated, and these, I think, will give his book a permanent place in the literature of nature.

The original edition of *Golden Days* included a prologue that the publishers have decided to omit – presumably because it dates a book that should be dateless. This prologue begins with the words: 'Today I have fished again in France.' It contains one passage that reveals Fedden's character much more closely than any words of mine:

'To-night there's starlight on the ghost towns. Still they lie, like grey bones on desert sands. Tonight the guns are thundering, and with each striking hour bleached desolation creeps further through the land … And when the end comes – as come it will for some of us – can we relive our golden days, lay hold upon reality, find simple kindly ways again? Or have we grown too old under the heel of might, inured to power, to speed, to all things obvious, tangible, moulded by concrete fact – stunned – bludgeoned by materialism? Must we pass hence only to leave this brazen god of ugliness triumphant?'

These words were written in 1918 when Fedden was serving with the British Expeditionary Force in France and when the First World War was not yet ended. By how many of us are they echoed today when the open spaces are shrinking with alarming speed and violence threatens from every side?

I write as a lover of this book with the hope that many readers will share my enthusiasm. Romilly Fedden, you will say, was an escapist from modern civilisation who was fortunate enough to be able to satisfy his desire. But he was no ordinary escapist. Like many silent men, he had learnt to think for himself. Hating materialism, he clung to the spiritual values of truth and goodness and beauty. He knew that they were to be found and refreshed, not in the hum and ugliness of cities, but in the quiet places and, above all, by the running streams which, symbolic of the life of man, begin as tiny trickles on the mountain side, until, twisting, burning and growing with every mile, they run down into the sea 'that leads everywhere, brings everything, and takes so much away.'

R. H. Bruce Lockhart
1948

AN APPRECIATION

Golden Days – Romilly Fedden (1875-1939)

Romilly Fedden was a large Englishman, a full six-foot-three, heavyset, with a slight stammer; he was a water-colourist of some stature by profession, a man reportedly of considerable wit and charm, and a confirmed cynic about most of the modern world; during World War I he was a captain in the British Expeditionary Force in France and thereafter became a pacifist who could say, echoing his close Breton friend Jean Pierre, 'I hate all governments.'

His watercolours still sell at auction and grace his wife Katherine's books, including one on the Basque country, and he wrote three books himself: *Modern Water-colour*, an interesting if not durable treatise on the art he practised; *Food and Other Frailties*, a perfectly charming celebration of food and wine that compares favourably with the best explorations of those subjects; and his brilliant, memorable, *Golden Days*, with the subtitle *From the Fishing Log of a Painter in Brittany.*

The latter was written in the tents and bivouacs of France during the First World War and then first published in 1919. It covers Fedden's extended stay, fishing and painting, that ended in 1913. The book has exceptional warmth and joy, great texture, and is filled with exciting and carefully recorded trips, meals, chances, stalkings and fights with fish – and one enduring friendship. It is all one might ask of a fishing memoir as much concerned with the quality of life and the place as with the details of angling.

This is not the dry-fly fishing of Plunket Greene or the intimate, gentle world of the British chalkstream. In fact, Fedden warns, 'There are two people who should not visit Brittany for the purposes of sport – the dry-fly purist, and his friend, the owner of fat parklands with stocked waters.' The fish in Brittany can be few and far between, but they are all wild; the pleasures will be in the wildness, the energy and excitement of a Breton village on market day, in Druid ruins, the character of local folk, the heather clad moors, rare meals and warm friendships, and yes, the unusual fishing can be exceptional at times in this severe, poor, rugged province in northwest France, on the Channel. It is 'not the place for the eager fisherman with only ten days at his disposal.'

The heart of *Golden Days* is the depth of feeling Fedden registers for his life in Brittany. In the prologue to the first edition, sadly not reprinted in the 1949 version, Fedden begins:

'Today I have fished again in France. Oh! But that sunlit hour was wonderful.' It is 1918 and the war is very much still on – for he hears the 'muffled thunder of the guns,' sees the silent searchlights in the night sky, catches the glint of a bayonet as troops move toward the front. He travels through a town he once knew well, now 'A ghost town that no words can paint – dark, horrible, and still,' what was once a 'human, kindly place.' And he asks if, when the end of the war comes, 'Can we relive our golden days?'

And that, without sentimentality, is what he does in his book.

Golden Days begins with a spring day, a trip in a wagon with the local mayor (and enough of the mayor's fine burgundy), a fully rigged expedition, and he captures what we all feel on such a day. 'I know, and you know,' he says, 'the delight of that moment when, for the first time in a season, one puts a rod together. Each click of the reel makes merry music. Winter is past! Spring is in the air and in our blood.'

With the eyes of the painter he is, he records the scents and sounds, the sights and shapes from rock to cloud, the water 'green and opalescent.'

All of his trips are expeditions, unhurried voyages into the landscapes and rivers of Brittany. Of a summer trip he says: 'There was fragrance everywhere, warm succulent scents of growing things, damp verdant mosses, wild raspberry, sorrel, musk and eglantine.' And the fishing can be delicious. 'The fish went down, so did my second sandwich,' he reports, watching the water while he eats. Then another fish is up and feeding, and 'it became a wild contest between ham sandwiches and Dark Olive Duns,' and he breaks off his own meal to try yet again, but the fish is 'too eager' and misses the fly. A little later there is a powerful thunderstorm and he seeks sanctuary in some Druid ruins, and a little later the sun is out 'on a golden world' and he misses a huge trout, takes a good one, and later insists that it be fried in 'the best of butter.' It is a day full of the 'extraordinarily exhilarating and unexpected.'

There is a fine section on flies and fly tying. He notes wisely that 'when dressing dry-flies we must always keep in mind the fish's point of view rather than our own.' And he makes shrewd observations on the importance of silhouette, the form by which we recognize all creatures, from giraffe to pig. 'Fineness and neatness,' he observes 'are important factors in the fly dresser's art, but not at the expense of character, transparency and correct tone.'

Throughout the book we experience one of the great friendships in fishing literature, with his Breton friend Jean Pierre, an expert on rivers and local folk lore, a man deft at worming and dapping, a wise and simple man and 'the most skilful fisherman in the countryside.'

It is Jean Pierre who is called to the war early and later rushed to Verdun to stem a night attack and killed by a bullet to his head.

Jean Pierre's strong, loyal, independent spirit pervades *Golden Days*, and his great beaver hat becomes a symbol of the best in Brittany. It is said that Fedden died in 1939 because he could no bear the thought of another world war.

Nick Lyons
Woodstock
New York
2011

BIOGRAPHICAL NOTE

Arthur Romilly Fedden was born in Henbury, Gloucester-shire, on 5th February 1875, one of the three sons of the Victorian artist Henry Fedden. Romilly studied painting at the School of Fine Arts in Hertford under Sir Hubert Herkomer and, later, under Jean-Paul Laurens at the École Nationale Superieure des Beaux-Arts in Paris.

In 1907 he married the American author, Katharine Waldo Douglas. They had one son, Robin Fedden (1908–1977), who was Middle East correspondent of the Financial Times, and author of several books on travel: *The Enchanted Mountains; Syria – An Historical Appreciation; English Travellers in the Near East* and an autobiography, *Chantemesle – A Normandy Childhood*.

Throughout his life Romilly Fedden travelled frequently in Spain and Portugal, in North Africa, and, of course, in France. His several long visits to Brittany, to Finistère and Morbihan, were the inspiration for his *chef-d'œuvre, Golden Days: From the Fishing-Log of a Painter in Brittany*.

Although he was nearly forty at the outbreak of the First World War, Fedden immediately joined up, serving first as a lieutenant, then captain, of the 11th Battalion, the Gloucestershire Regiment. These were traumatic years for him, from which he took a long time to recover.

In 1917 he published *Modern Water-colour: including Some Chapters on Current-Day Art*, in which he describes his painting techniques. He illustrated several of his wife's

books and writings: in 1904 an article dedicated to the Isle
of Capri in the art review, The Studio; in 1921, a travel book,
The Basque Country, and in 1933 *Manor Life in Old France*.
Romilly Fedden continued to paint prolifically throughout
his life. Some of his paintings are in the Victoria and Albert
Museum in London, as well as at several museums and
galleries in Bristol, Manchester and Liverpool; the Bristol
Museum has one of his best-known works, *Pastorale
Bretonne*. He also regularly held exhibitions of his work in
the UK – for example, he exhibited 105 paintings at the Goupil
Gallery, and as many as 432 at the Walker Gallery in London!

Unfortunately Fedden's diaries have never been found
so we know little of his private life beyond what he tells us
in his books. We do know that he was a great admirer of
Charles Condor (1868–1909), the Impressionist painter of
the Glasgow school, who lived in Chantmesle, near Haut-
Isle-sur-la-Seine in France. Fedden, together with a friend,
had a commemorative plaque erected in his memory. Then,
around 1921, Romilly Fedden and his wife moved into
Condor's house. By all accounts the Feddens' home was
warm, welcoming and refined. Romilly was a man of culture,
a connoisseur of wine and a lover of fine food. He wrote and
illustrated a book, *Food and Other Frailties* (published in
1948, several years after his death), which reveals his great
love of all things French.

On 29th March 1939 Romilly and Katherine Fedden were
returning to France from Spain when the Madrid-Paris
Express was wrecked near Beasain in Spain. Romilly died at
once, and Katherine died from her injuries a few weeks later.
They are buried in the old cemetery at Saint-Jean-de-Luz.

Claude Belloir
Pommerit le Vicomte
Brittany
2008

ACKNOWLEDGEMENTS

I am indebted to Claude Belloir for permission to base the Biographical Note on the Introduction to his beautifully translated 2008 *Editions de Trieux* edition of *Golden Days*.

Two old friends have sung the praises of Romilly Fedden for many years, and have both contributed to this edition: Nick Lyons and Geoffrey Bucknall, both anglers and writers of great wisdom, and both connoisseurs of literature and lovers of France. I value their opinions very highly and am honoured that they have chosen to be associated with this edition.

I was very pleased to make contact with Romilly Fedden's granddaughter, Katherine Fedden, and Romilly's great-grandson, Yacine M'Seffar, a keen flyfisherman. Both have been very helpful, particularly in making available Romilly's painting of trout flies which Yacine has photographed so skilfully.

I have long been familiar with Terence Lambert's beautiful painting of a kingfisher looking down at a trout; a print of it hangs above the fly-tying bench of my fishing companion Emyr Lewis, so I see it frequently. One of the joys of being a publisher is having the opportunity to bring together the disparate skills of the different people involved. In this case my colleague Paul Curtis and designer Pete Mackenzie combined Terence's glorious image, redolent of summer, with the dark stark image of a First World War battlefield to produce an image that reflects the contrasts found in *Golden Days*.

I am grateful to the Imperial War Museum for permission to reproduce the battlefield image.

Most of all, of course, I am grateful to Romilly Fedden himself, for leaving us that most delectable of angling books, *Golden Days: From the Fishing-Log of a Painter in Brittany.*

Paul Morgan
Machynlleth
2011

FOREWORD

The famous Finnish composer, Jean Sibelius, was in his garden in the company of a music critic who had been somewhat unkind about the composer's recent symphony. A blackbird greeted him with its melodious warbling. The critic cried out: 'Ah, that's what I call a true musician.' The blackbird's song was suddenly cut short by the harsh croaking of a carrion crow. 'And that,' riposted Sibelius, 'is his music critic!'

This incident came to mind when I was asked to write this Foreword to Romilly Fedden's book, *Golden Days*. The publisher finds a reader who really loves the book. He asks him (or her) to write a sincere appreciation. The editor of a consumer product, the angling magazine, may well do the opposite, to choose someone whom he knows to be antagonistic to the author to write a book review. Thus for an hour or two, by dipping his pen into sour grape juice, the reviewer seeks to demolish up to three years of the author's blood, sweat and tears. And at the same time he imposes the stamp of his own mediocre talent on the new book.

I prefer to write a Foreword. I recall that I have only written one book review in a long life as an angling scribe. During that time the reading habits of the angling public had changed, and in changing, they also changed the demands of the market place. It is probable that today Romilly Fedden would have had to hawk his manuscript from door to door of reluctant publishers. Yet, when asked some years ago by the *Fly Fisher's Journal* to choose my own Desert Island book, without any quibble I cited Romilly Fedden's *Golden Days*, even though it was little sought after, save by appreciative collectors.

Here I must apologise, for having passed my eighty year milepost, I have no need to make an ego trip. My own early autobiography, *Fishing Days*, was the link to what became my own personal favourite fishing book. It happened that long, long ago my publisher asked me to help promote my book at a London literary event. An elderly man came up to me. He was clutching a book with a blue hard cover. He confessed to having enjoyed my own book. He introduced himself as a director of the famous publishing house of A. & C. Black. He gave me the copy of Fedden's *Golden Days*, saying that my own writing showed that I had much in common with its author.

At first I thought we were not much alike. Fedden was a tall man and I was short. He was a recognised artist whereas I had no such talent. But when I turned the pages I came to recognise a kindred spirit. We were both Francophiles even though France and Brittany after the Great War had changed the almost tourist-free landscape of Old Brittany beyond recognition. We both detested Authority. We did not seek 'to maintain standards'. In short, Fedden was a rebellious spirit, and so am I.

Now we come to the quality of writing. It can be summed up in that word 'style'. It is not enough to produce complex sentences where meaning drowns in a surfeit of adjectives. One angling writer bravely plunges into a complex sentence, then fights his way through a welter of subordinate clauses, a habit he inherited from Victorian prose. There are such books; they exasperate the reader. Fedden avoids this temptation. He has a uniquely disciplined style.

He uses the right amount of language. You can almost smell the blue-smoke mist through which the ambulances carry the wounded soldiers back from the Front Line. Fedden and his boon companion, the rustic poacher, Jean Pierre, share the dog cart which takes them both to the railway station, and to war. They drive along the moonlit lane, past the chapel to Saint Herbot where Romilly had his studio. Fedden would join his regiment and return from war. Jean Pierre would die from a German bullet at Verdun. Their way of life – and much more – ended at that train station, but not before Jean Pierre had waved his whip at the night sky, crying, 'I hate Governments. How I hate them.'

That same dogcart would have taken a jolly party to the streams that traversed *les landes*. There was the mayor, chuckling, rubbing his hands together in the chill of the early morning. The Notary would conceal a sly smile as he had also concealed a box of worms. Jean Pierre was thinking that he would wind a sliver of lead foil around his Invicta fly to make it sink into the deep pools. They would return in the evening with the spoils of the chase. The trout would be fried in butter and washed down with local cider…

… But here I must resist temptation. Only a sadist would reveal to you in advance the glorious adventures of this joyous party. There will be the one-upmanship of Romilly, with the skills he brought from England's chalkstreams. Can he match the poaching wiles of Jean Pierre? Then, in the evening, when the velvet night falls across the countryside and the wind rattles the cottage shutters Jean Pierre will chill the blood of his listeners with tales of the ghoulies and ghosties which roam the land after sundown. At last, as they shiver, he smiles and says, '*on dit ça mais …*' and they all join in his laughter.

No, I will not spoil your future enjoyment as you turn the pages of my favourite book of fishing stories. My copy is a first edition, published in 1919, just after the great guns fell silent. And Romilly joined the Great Majority before the guns began to speak again in 1939. Those years between the wars must have been sadness for him. Brittany had lost its young sons in Flanders' fields.

The hedonistic tourists of the inter-war years invaded the sunken lanes. Exhaust fumes hung in the air between the high hedges. They discovered the secret streams. Would they have revealed that partly ruined chapel dedicated to Saint Herbot, the saint who was devoted to the care of the dumb beasts of the farmers' fields? Beyond Brittany he is scarcely recognised.

Today the Cosmologists assure us that Time runs only in one direction. It races ahead with the expanding Universe. We cannot return to one man's golden days.

Each of us has one's own golden days. Mine were two years of boyhood when my mother left my father. She took me to live with her in a converted railway carriage in a tiny hamlet on the Romney Marsh. My small world was encompassed by sinuous eels and the shining roach shoals in the Royal Military Canal. Yes, I had much in common with Romilly Fedden, for my golden days, too, were shattered by war.

So I close my eyes. I am half-dozing by the fire of a winter's night. The last drops of Rémy-Martin have dried in the bottom of my glass. For a moment, somewhere between waking and sleeping, I have proved the Cosmologists to be wrong. I can hear the dogcart's wheels grind on the gravel. The horses go *clopin-clopant* along that moonlit ribbon. I am with the jolly party returning from the stream. We pass cottage windows, aglow from candles and oil lamps. Then we go by the whitewashed walls of St. Herbot's Chapel. Yes, the dear friend I never met was Romilly Fedden. He did change the rules of the Universe for me. He reverses time for his readers to relive short moments in Old Brittany. Romilly, your Brittany book is alive again, and well.

So if ever Society would be wise enough to maroon my

rebellious spirit, here is one book I would crave for. At home, in bed, I have but to stretch out my hand to find this book. Once I had a large collection of fishing books. Through a mistake, I had bought them from my loan account money I had invested in my business. In 1992 I retired and closed my shop, little realising that technically the books belonged to the business and not to me. I was a limited liability company.

I had instructed a professional firm to close down my business, for I paid off all my debts … but they claimed the books as part of the stock. Yet I took one for myself. I was not bitter. I am not an obsessive collector by nature. I remembered the sacred words my grandmother had called to me often enough: 'Geoffrey, shut the bloody door after you when you go out!' And so I did, but with one hand still clutching my favourite book which you, too, Dear Reader, will be able to enjoy. I shall own it even to the time when I hear 'the Porter's shoulder-knot a-creaking.'

Geoffrey Bucknall
Lartington,
Barnard Castle,
County Durham
August 2010

(Frontispiece drawing of 'Jean Pierre')

From a drawing by S. Curnow Vosper, R.W.S.

PROLOGUE

B.E.F., France, 1918.

*T*ODAY *I have fished again in France!*
Oh! But that sunlit hour was wonderful! Only those who have endured these weary times will fully understand – to find forgetfulness! And I had found much more – a wealth of old attachment, the mystery of the river, keen scents, soft well-remembered sounds, clean sunlight and the greenness of the valley, even a friendly miller, quite like a Breton, save that he did not wear a beaver hat – such a good fellow too, kindly, gesticulating, uttering the strange new language of these times: 'No bon' this pool; I must come down and fish his meadow; that signboard on the hedge with its scrawled 'pêche reservée', that was 'no bon' too. In fact it did not count – or only 'pour les Boches – compre?'

The miller left me to contented solitude. This pool 'no bon' indeed! Why, already I had taken and returned two fish, both bright if undersized; and there was still a big one who cruised and sucked continually beneath the spreading thorn!

The fairy seed of the thistledown tiptoed from pool to pool. Among the weeds the dabchicks clucked contentedly. I sat in the long grass expectant, and fastened on an olive-dun. I pulled the wings apart and started oiling... while on the air there came a droning sound, faint but growing – surely no voice of river midge could thus break crystal silence... even a bumble-bee... Then up on the hill above the anti-aircrafts opened out – the shriek of shells resounded down the valley. They could not touch the faint grey speck that floated in the blue, high above white bursts of shrapnel. Only the fairy spell was broken, its glamour gone – one fell a-thud to thoughts of wreck and ruin, to madness, ugliness and pain; to dust-choked roads, crowded with sweat-stained, grim-faced men; to the weariness of their marching... What right had I to golden-houred oblivion in such times as these? Then under the thorn bush came again a 'plop with following circle, as if to say good-bye. But I did not regret that old trout a bit. Thank heaven that he still lives! – only a Mills bomb could take him in his fastness... Besides, we had both had our little bit of fun; each realised that patch of starwort weed five yards below his tail – a sure and certain sanctuary.

So from the short-lived peace of water meadows I turned to glaring highroad, where in the dust the endless lorries passed. Beyond, the camp, the incinerator's reek, the trampled horse-lines, the petrol-cans, the dumps. The guard tent, its barbed encircling wires; the canteen's ugliness, the odour of stale beer, the rag-smeared tables and the flies. Then came the village, with its ruined church, its broken crucifix, its sightless lath-lined windows; its one small shop where you can buy 'silk-cards', eggs, and sometimes chocolate. On again up to the crossroads, where on your right you meet a one-time farm. Behind it you will find a big green orchard.

In the evening light this seemed inviting – there at the further end a tent, its flaps flung wide to candlelight that glimmered on its white spread table. Here we dined well, thanks to the A.S.C., likewise our good host's cook, who can disguise even 'Maconochie'... Below, the bugle notes rang out – faint and fainter down the valley. Afterwards the orderlies arranged our chairs, with coffee and liqueurs, under the apple-trees; while overhead the searchlights stared unceasingly, projecting beams of silent light, sweeping to close and hold a fleck of silver cloud, and then move on...

Our car is waiting, its great head-lights call us, guiding a way between the trunks of apple-trees... We glide through the ruined village, past the sleeping camp, its tents now grey and silent – on up the winding road, higher and higher, then open country, a vast tableland. Darkness behind us. Eastward the far-flung skyline slashed with unnatural light, the glare that ebbs and flows unceasingly, the distant star-shells points of floating flame, the muffled thunder of the guns.

The sound grows nearer. We touch the fringe of desolation – heaped ruin that was once a human, kindly place. Just one – resembling countless others. A ghost town, that no words can paint – dark, horrible, and still, beneath the stars. The throbbing of the guns can only punctuate this silence. The sightless streets seem endless, monotonous, their ranked lines of rubble-heap. All is unreal, fantastic, benumbed with world-pain. This ghost town has no house, only stark things of stone and gaping beam that strike against the sky.

Our way lies through the main square. There we must bear to the right. (You remember the little barbers shop upon the corner?) Tonight there is no square, but only desert space, marked out by piles of battered masonry – no living creature but one hungry cat, who slinks into the shadows.

We leave this place, passing between the pockmarked banks – by countless dug-outs, blank, torn holes, where countless men have suffered more than death. Dead are the trees too, prone, lopped along the way with tangled wire, rotting equipment, tattered camouflage, and all the sordid wrack of war. Dim in the starlight stands a little wooden cross. Its top is roofed, just in the way that peasants form their wayside calvaries in Southern Germany. A dead horse lies beneath it in a ditch.

Ahead of us are lights! The main road – military police. Here we must stop to let the 'heavies' pass. They lumber on into the night. Beyond them a bayonet flashes; grey-coated figures are passing – marching westward. The murmur of the guns grows faint – then dies away.

The road races past us like a moving tape, unfolding endless lines of poplars, the gleam of whitewash on a wayside farm, a church-crowned hamlet with its echoing street, a hasty glint on its mysterious windows; then pollard-trees again. Our way runs on to dip, through gloom, to leafy solitudes; mile upon mile of forest – no human habitation here; soundless too, save for our engine's measured throb. The dark woods deepen; only the car's edge is cut clear by our headlamps' glow; above, the treetops black against the sky. The rest is vague, mysterious, with cool moss-scented airs from deep wet glades where toadstools grow. Here surely there is peace untouched and still sequestered. Look up…!A red ball falls beyond the wood edge. The signal lights flash out – they are moving fast... The air is vibrant with their deep-toned humming... Our bombing planes flock home, their night's work done.

Now in my billet the lamp is lit, the curtains are close drawn. Before me on the table lie some sheets of pencilled foolscap that should have been the Preface to this book. I took some trouble with those pencil notes! Their vein was light – nay, almost jocular. They seemed to me a fitting Apologia – indeed, quite charming in their dainty touch, on fishing days and fairies in 'a legend-crusted land'.

Tonight there's starlight on the ghost towns! Still they lie, like grey bones on desert sands. Tonight the guns are thundering, and with each striking hour bleached desolation creeps further through the land...

And when the end comes – as come it will for some of us – can we relive our golden days? Lay hold upon reality? Find simple, kindly ways again? Or have we grown too old under the heel of might, inured to power, to speed, to all things obvious, tangible, moulded by concrete fact – stunned – bludgeoned by materialism?

Must we pass hence only to leave this brazen god of ugliness triumphant?

The pencilled sheets of foolscap still lie untouched upon my table. Doubtless this book needs adequate apology. Yet shall it claim but one excuse – its writer's love of Brittany. Because of this I may perhaps stir here and there some slender cord of sympathy; make others love it too. To me this would be good, to thus find unknown friends – so, as it were, touch hands, if only for a moment, across the far-dividing plains of chance and circumstance.

The dawn is breaking. In the blue mist below my window the ambulances pass slowly – one by one.

CHAPTER I

A SPRING FISHING

It is always worthwhile to keep a fishing log, for reasons apart from its value as a reference of tactics or record of bare facts. It is always a pleasure to turn back its pages and so relive the past. Would it not be delightful in these leaden times, if we might carry our friends along with us, back to those golden days! Would they understand, or would there be some who; when they saw us going a-fishing, merely thought we went a-catching fish? It is the spirit of fishing we would here emphasise, its immeasurable charm and mystery which ever leads us to green and flower-girt pastures, on beyond the leafy woods, where wild birds sing. Never can we reach our final goal, for always before us lie further fields yet to explore. Skill and experience may take us far, but beyond are Jenny Spinners and all the flies we have as yet not learned to tie! If we have acquired some wisdom in those diverse doings of the river's underworld, we then begin to understand how much is still to learn. We may have studied the ways of bulgers with the nymphs, or even found a fit device to tackle tailers. We may have stalked successfully a few gut-shy trout, yet still we know there are as good fish in the water meadow as ever came out of it – and better.

Above all, there is the indefinable thrill of things concerning open skies, unfettered solitudes, misty dawns, and dewy twilights, the sights and sounds and fragrance along the river-bank, the first mayfly of the season, the scent of leather that pervades an old and well-worn fly-book, within, the same familiar faces, wreathed with gut-strands dry and brittle, outrageously behackled, decked out with faded jay and jungle-cock. For the most part they are idle drones who never took a single fish; but there is one, a lean old Marquis, a keen sportsman in his day, now barbless and bedraggled, yet a proud fly still. These rarely walk beside the river with us now, but bide at home in their snug, mellow parchment, dozing upon a shelf beside the studio fire.

There are, too, those blank days, which then seemed tragedies, wherein we toiled and worried just missed. There are those farmhouse teas – the fortifying cake and jam that, reviving futile hopes, encouraged us to go out and try again.

Of course, being human, we all like to catch fish; and yet, is it not the desire to catch rather than the catching which is more than half the fun? You remember that evening when at the mill bridge we took our rods apart? Our creels were not too heavy. Just below us in the meadow rabbits came out to frisk and take supper in the evening light; across the river the willow-trees loomed big, the mists were stealing up the valley... Lord! What a long walk home we had... And that day in June, that glorious sweltering day, when all the fish came short – yet not quite all, we got two brace between us – that was a big fish on the specially tied Mayfly which broke you in the run below the hatch-hole. Then our lunch – you remember? Under the apple trees in the orchard? Those red ants in the ginger beer; my hard boiled egg was bad... That was a good day too.

In selecting dates from the Breton diary, one is prompted by an egotism, more or less unconscious, to pick out only the red-letter days when all went well, so to hand on to one's friends the bags that were disproportionately heavy – or should we say less light than usually was the case? I would try, however, only to touch on days which possibly may be of some small help to other fishermen, remembering

also the insuperable difficulty of giving more than a slight
impression of each picture as I see it.

Dinner had finished at the Lion d'Or. Anastasie had just
filled the coffee glasses, and placed the *cafetière* on the open
hearth. The Greffier was pouring out an ample *fine maison*,
and his voluble discourse on fish and fishing brought him
finally to the mill at Trestrenou. I was lighting my pipe when
the proposal was broached. His cousin, it seemed, was the
miller, and his river far-famed among the fishers of Morbihan.
True, it was a long journey, some twenty kilometres by road,
and the Lion d'Or boasted no carriage. But then, again,
Monsieur le Maire had often expressed a wish to go a-fishing,
so we would invite Monsieur le Maire and drive in his cart.
And had I tasted the Mayor's old burgundy? He smacked his
lips, and blew a kiss as only a Frenchman can. Of course
we must take a hamper with our *dejeuner* – tomorrow?
Tomorrow would be excellent – that is, if I could tear myself
for a day from my glorious art. I could! Tant mieux. Once a
fisherman, always a fisherman. Then nothing would serve
but that Anastasie should go and present many compliments
to Monsieur le Maire; and would he, perhaps, step across
and join us in a 'night cap' to discuss an affair of the most
important?

Ten minutes later the Mayor arrived – a stout, kindly
little man, wearing a tailcoat and a bowler hat a size too
small. I never remember seeing him without this hat;
indeed, I think his only claim to office was his good heart,
his un-Breton raiment, and maybe his ample supply of this
world's goods, among which his cellar was not least. He
was enchanted with our proposal, and fell in with all the
Greffier's suggestions, beaming upon us, and rubbing his
little fat hands together. Everything would arrange itself
perfectly. Might he do himself the honour of seeing to the
hamper? And did Monsieur like burgundy? *Eh bien*, there

should be burgundy. Jean Pierre should bring the carriage to our door. That was understood? *Bien!* And he beamed and rubbed his hands again. The whole company in the inn kitchen had drawn their chairs into the circle round the fire. The Greffier and the Mayor sat on each side of the hearth, talking and gesticulating like excited schoolboys. They had, in fact, fished this river together in their youth, and each in his turn must now cap the other's stories of trout vaster and vaster in waters more and more delectable. It was late when I left my friends and lighted my candle. It was later still when I snuggled down between the coarse Breton sheets after a lingering and hopeful preparation of rod and tackle. After all, it is the anticipation in fishing which is more than half the fun; and those casts soaked in the water jug overnight may create an enthusiasm that will carry us to the end of a dull day's fishing on the morrow.

Next morning I stepped into a sun shiny world to find the village street in contented bustle. The preparations for the weekly market were in full swing. Unharnessed carts with green hoods filled the inn yard, and from the square came sounds of beating mallets. Booths were being erected. Hens, ducks, and farmers' wives were all noisily loquacious. Our conveyance was already at the door, dogs barking at the horse's head, while Jean Pierre was endeavouring to stow a substantial hamper under the front seat. My old friend, Jean Pierre, is here simply introduced as the quondam coachman of Monsieur le Maire, but I like to remember him as the best of good fellows, an inveterate poacher and the most skilful fisherman in the countryside.

His master soon arrived, swathed in a voluminous lambskin coat – the early morning was still chill – wearing the inevitable bowler hat, and carrying a huge bundle of nets and rods.

A start from a Breton village on such an occasion is always a lengthy business. The Greffier was still in the inn garden,

seeking to replenish his stock of lobworms. Then the local
chemist must needs run across with a bottle of physic, which
we would please deposit at the farm of Kestrec en route. This
led to an altercation as to which was our best road, till, finally,
maps were produced, and after great discussion, in which a
deputation of half the village took an active part, the point of
dispute was eventually settled, and amidst a chorus of good
wishes we clattered through the marketplace and out on to
the high road. There are scant cushions and poor springs to
a Breton cart, and a long drive can be a stiff and cramping
experience. I was not sorry when we climbed the last hill
and found ourselves amongst stunted oaks, grey rocks, and
heather-clad moors, with open country stretching away on
either side. We were on the Breton *landes*, which still hold
the fey spirit of ancient Cornouaille. A tract of solitude,
under low skies, dotted here and there with Druid stones,
which, like the graves of the martyrs in the grey Galway
land, stand cold and lonely in infinite sadness. But below
us the sun was shining, and friendly sounds, very thin yet
distinct, rose from the valley in the morning air. A peasant
was singing from somewhere down below, and then came
the intermittent bleating of sheep mingling with the faint
tinkling of their bells. And there was the river! It lay well
down in the midst of orchards and green fields, interspersed
with patches of foliage and broken uncultivated land.

We pulled up at the bridge, for here we would start fishing.
Jean Pierre was to take the horse and cart with our hamper
by a grass track to the mill, some distance farther down the
valley.

I know, and you know, the delight of that moment when,
for the first time in a. season, one puts a rod together! Each
click of the reel makes merry music. Winter is past! Spring
is in the air and in our blood. Perhaps our pleasure reaches
its height when, cast in mouth, we mark the first circle of
the coming rise, and then select the fly on which the fish will

soon be feeding. Today no hatch of fly was visible, so, putting up a tentative Blue Dun, I started off to explore some likely looking pools above the bridge.

What a morning it was! A heron flew up like a ghost from the shallows at the bend of the stream, and from the farther bank, through willows and poplars, the slanting sunlight dappled the landscape in blue and gold. Here and there grey clusters of rock showed stark amidst the gorse, and farther up the hillside spring buds were purple. The woods were awake. High overhead a lark was singing. Magpies chattered in a near thicket. The river clattered over a gravel bed, and then chuckled as it found a deep brown pool below. There was only one note missing from the symphony – that reiterated plump, plump, so pleasant to the ear of a fisherman, accompanied by that oily bubble in the shadow of the far bank, and those widening circles on the water which denote a feeding trout.

Not a fish had shown itself, and, naturally, a floating fly was useless. I had changed a wet fly many times to no purpose, and was now fishing down stream, sinking my line as much as possible, and exploring each eddy and likely hole as I reached it. Though I worked ceaselessly, not a touch did I get. The fish were evidently quite off the feed; the banks in many places were flooded; my feet were wet, and I was cold and rather disheartened. The glint had gone out of the sunlight. The magpie's note seemed now ironical. Surely they realised the absurdity of throwing an artificial bunch of feathers to catch a visionary fish. Those cackling birds were cursed as I slowly climbed the steep hillside, the water squelching in my boots at every step. Under a *menhir* stone I took them off. Here, at least, was a suntrap where tobacco would taste good. Young ferns made a comfortable resting place on which to lie full length and philosophise on the unimportance of an empty creel. After all it might have been much worse, for little fleecy clouds sailed high aloft, warm airs played through my clothing from head to foot and caressed me into a mood of forgetfulness. Gradually the colour returned to the sunlight. Pan was out in the woods again and shouting joyously from the splash of gorse on the hillside; a little faint haze lay among the tall and slender ash stems in the hollow, where the water slept green and opalescent in deep pools between the willows. From farther up I could hear from time to time the sound of chopping wood. It was good to lie here in the warmth, limbs relaxed, the open sky above. My hands in cushioning my head must have crushed wild thyme, for its fragrance crept round and enveloped me. Not only scent but, sound and sight, became very close and intimate. The chopping had ceased, and now another voice became apparent from across the valley – a tinkle of flowing water over a gravel bed. Leaning on my elbow, I found it out. Not the main river this, but a small upland stream bubbling into the larger water by way of reedy marshes. Its glint shone clear through the pinewood on the farther bank, was lost in a withy copse, and then showed itself again, a ribbon of silver threading the brown heather of the distant moorland; probably too small to hold many trout, but what fun to explore and see!

While putting on my boots, the woodcutter came into view carrying a huge bundle of faggots. We fell into talk, a curious *argot*, half French, half Breton. No, the fishing was never good in this river; but today it must be useless with the wind in the very worst quarter (all fishermen know this remark by heart). Monsieur has caught nothing – well, that is all that can be expected with the water up high. Monsieur intends to try the freshet across the valley? Pure waste of time, and, moreover, a tiresome walk round by the way up the mill. Why, only last summer that watercourse was as dry as a bone, never a single fish had he, the woodcutter, ever taken there. No, if I must fish, the main stream was my sole chance. The old fellow looked down his nose as he discoursed on the futility of that little brook, and there and then I made a secret resolve to explore it at all costs. I left the old man muttering pessimisms, and sauntered down to the riverbank again, casting here and there a desultory fly in likely comers. Soon I was joined by Jean Pierre with a message that *déjeuner* would be awaiting me at the mill. I was now using a good-sized Invicta, fishing it as wet as possible, but with very little hope of moving a fish. My old friend followed me down the bank, and eventually we arrived at the mill bridge. I had just reeled in my line when my eye wandered to a pool lower down the stream. Surely that was the splash of a fish just below the overhanging alder bush; anyway, I would have just one last cast, and try just one more pool before I went in. Brothers of the rod all know that final cast, and will remember the lure of that further stretch of water which has been responsible for many lost fish, lost trains, lost dinners, and lost tempers. Down the bank we went, and there under the alder sat a good-sized water rat brushing his whiskers. Jean Pierre was fumbling for his leather snuff pouch, and at his movement the little beast dived, giving us an exact facsimile of the splash I had seen a few moments before. Now Jean, having taken his pinch of snuff, also extracted from his pouch a piece of lead, and began, with the aid of his clasp knife, peeling from it a long thin strip. This, with three or four neat turns, he fastened round the shank of my fly. So was I tempted, and fell. After all, the fish were not near the surface, and if the river held a single trout this was the only possible way to lure him from the bottom. I was now casting well down stream, working my fly up and across the current. At the third cast the line tightened. I struck, and found myself fast in a good fish. By keeping a severe strain on him we avoided some dangerous-looking snags at the tail of the pool; then the fish turned suddenly – there was a perilous second of slack line till he came fighting hard into deep water. Three times did Jean Pierre stand by with the net, and three times were those wild upstream rushes repeated.

At last the fish came slowly in on its side, a dark fin showing. The net was dexterously slipped under him, and we had him safely on the bank – a good fish, if rather dark in colour, and well over two pounds. So we came to the mill, Jean Pierre and the trout proudly heading the procession.

The old mill kitchen seemed dark, at first as we came in from the strong light, but soon one realised its warmth of colour and its air of comfort. Gradually things began to take form in this big living room. There was a glint of brass and pewter on the long, low dresser by the open hearth; curtains of red hung over the old wooden beds built into the wall, with bright green blankets for coverlets. The floor was of beaten earth, a glorified ladder of age-worn oak led to the loft, above. The only modern touch was a deep window built, into the old wall at the far end of the room, and through this the sunlight glistened on a massive table. Here the Greffier was carving cold woodcock, while the Mayor, in shirtsleeves, was mixing a salad with infinite precision. Soon we were all partaking of a royal luncheon. It was a gay party, everyone talking at once. The miller himself had lunched an hour earlier, but he must come and sit beside us, and sample the famous burgundy. The fowls, meanwhile, were hunting for crumbs, and softly clucking to each other around the table. Then a convivial and very large pig joined the party, till he was stampeded, grunting in outraged dudgeon by our host's *sabot*. Above me, enshrined in a niche in the opposite wall, stood St. Herbot, an ancient saint in faience, of forbidding countenance. His china face seemed to take on a fierce expression as through glazed eyes he glowered at all the good dishes below. But this was not our West Country, at home, where a fisher can lunch on an austere hunk of bread and cheese. There had been no substantial Devonshire breakfast of ham and eggs, clotted cream, and honey. The early dawn had only brought one bowl of *café au lait*, so now a second cut of the Camembert cheese became a delicious necessity. After came strong black coffee, borne to us on a tray by the young goddess Yvonne. And what can I say of Yvonne? She who heaped fresh branches on the fire, and stood, white-coiffed, by the hearthstone smiling; I do not even know if she was the daughter of the miller, or simply the maid of the mill. She remains an unknown divinity, bronzed, tall, full-girdled, and very beautiful. Perhaps her figure was a trifle ample, and her arms a little red and overdeveloped, but her eyes were of the deep seas. Under level brows she regarded us impartially, and ever that inimitable smile of mystery on her lips. Her mouth was made to kiss little children, and its subtle curve might drive men mad. Indeed, the Greffier burst into poetry, surpassing himself in a running fire pf gallantry, but the goddess only dimpled benignly, and bore him a live brand from off her altar wherewith to light his pipe. What must her voice have been with that deep breast and full column of a throat? We never heard it, and only St. Herbot knows if she was wise or simply very stupid.

But Monsieur le Maire was talking. His polite French indicated that in plain English my victim of the fly was a beastly fluke. I examined my coffee cup, and tried not to remember a length of twisted lead. Jean Pierre took a pinch of snuff, and chuckled. It seemed my only chance of a good bag was to take to the worm in the afternoon. Why, there had been not a trace of a hatch of fly all day; in fact, the Mayor was prepared to lay any odds against successful fly fishing under present conditions.

I quite believed him, but I also remembered that old woodcutter and my secret purpose to explore a little stream some half-mile up the valley. If chance should take us in different directions, we arranged that we should all eventually meet at the bridge.

We parted with mutual good wishes for 'tight lines,' and I made my way along the hillside, dipped down through the withy plantation below, and came out through a lichen-covered gate on to rough country bordering my little stream. It was, in fact, a Hampshire river in miniature, golden gravelled, clear as crystal, but so small that at most places one could take it at a jump. As I peered over the bank a good trout backed like a phantom into obscurity. He had seen me. But there were fish in the stream! In the next run above I marked rings in the shadow of a reed bed. There was a hatch of fly gaily sailing down the ripple. With my landing net I ladled for a specimen, and eventually secured one – a small dark midge. There was no black fly small enough in my case, but a small Black Gnat with wings cut off made a sufficient replica. This was soon touched up with paraffin and attached to my lightest cast. Then began that first moment of adventure, which is, perhaps, most delightful in retrospect and from the chimney corner. To the average human being the actual experience is altogether too critical. He finds himself with curiously tremulous knees, fishing hurriedly and very badly, catching his line in each overhanging branch, and convinced that every moment will bring the rise to an end. It was no easy fishing this in water clear as gin, where the slightest 'drag' put the fish down; but there were plenty of fly up, and the trout were feeding! A circle in the shadow, the fly floating free a foot above, and at once a fish had it. On this fine gear he gave me all the fun I wanted, the chief trouble being to work him downstream, and so avoid those sudden rushes up which would disturb other feeding fish above. From pool to pool one trout after another came safely to the net. And what trout they were! Not big fellows, but short and stocky, and all of them a good quarter of a pound, as beautiful fish as I have ever seen.

Above me the river took a sharp bend, and beneath a clump of dock leaves I noted a dimple on the slowly moving water. All the rises I had hitherto marked had been more noisy and pretentious. Here, perhaps, was a heavier fish. Stalking on

all fours, I made my first cast at least a yard too short; my
second attempt was equally unfortunate, for my line caught
on a bramble and produced a nasty drag. I waited, watching
that clump of weeds till the ripples on the water began again.
The third cast was more successful. The shadow of a dock
leaf dimpled, and I was fast in a good fish.

I like to think he was well over the pound; in any case, he
was much heavier than anything taken during the afternoon,
and fought like a tiger. In my excitement, I put on an extra
ounce of strain as he pulled and bored for a deep hole. There
was a plunge, and my cast returned unto me fly-less.

Well, there were other good fish in the stream, so I felt
for my fly box, sitting down the while on the bank side to
manipulate a second gnat. Before starting on again I laid
out my catch on the mossy peat, and thanked heaven and
the sunlight that I was here, and not dangling a lobworm in
that dreary river down the valley. Kingcups were growing
beside the bank, and with them I lined my creel, making a lit
resting-place for my five brace of brightly spotted little fish,
all of a size, and each as fat as butter.

Then I started off again, and worked on up the water,
taking a fish here and there. By the time I had reached the
open moorland it was late afternoon, a golden haze lay over
the river, and the runs between the pools were molten.

The trout were still feeding, but the fishing had become
more difficult, for the moorland lay with shoulders hunched
over the little stream. Here sound became more useful than
sight in detecting a rise; in fact, it was a game of 'hide-and-
seek'. A splash located the fish, and then began endless
attempts to get the fly past the overhanging banks and
down to the water below. Once there, wet or dry, the fish
usually took it. Curiously enough, the trout in these narrow
gullies were larger than in the more open water below, and
my last brace must have together weighed over the pound.
I followed up the windings of the stream, and eventually

found myself on a disused track which forded the shallows, and there, marked by a line of stunted oaks, stretched into the distance. I came to a standstill, aware of a sense of loss and change. The sound of feeding fish had ceased, the glint of the sunlight had vanished, giving place to a creeping mist, which moved like a pall above the waters. Before me the silent moors stretched endlessly away. Only those who have known the Breton *landes* at twilight can realise their drear melancholy, with something in it that is sinister, an echo of the underworld. Across the valley the note of a bittern sounded like a human cry. No wonder the peasants walk many leagues round rather than cross this track after sundown. I confess my pace quickened while passing a *menhir*, which loomed big in the half-light. Here Druids had offered sacrifice. Surely that was a dwarfed, crouching figure by the stone?

With my inward eye 'tis an old man grey,
With my outward, a thistle across the way.

With an effort I stood still. To break the spell I tried to shout a cheerful halloa. The sound came back derisively. As I listened the murmur of the ford was borne to me loud and distinct, then hushed again by the silent fingers of the evening breeze. I called to mind Jean Pierre's stories of the Washers of the Ford, and hurried on again, listening to fancied footsteps that followed faster and faster behind me. Of course it was absurd, and a sudden bolt in' this country would only result in a fall, and possibly a sprained ankle.

It was a long walk back. Twice I tried a short cut, only to find myself in bog land or thick undergrowth, and each time must needs return to the stream bank and follow its windings down to the plain. Darkness had quite fallen when I reached the pine wood, through which I stumbled, very content to see the carriage lamp glimmering ahead on the bridge.

Here, the others awaited me. The Mayor had already taken his place on the driving seat, while the Greffier was packing in the rods and tackle preparatory to our start. They both asked questions together. Had I lost my way in the dark? Had I obtained any sport? The fishing was not what it used to be, and today quite impossible for *la mouche*, but I had persisted in attempting the impossible. It was a pity I had not come down to the water below the mill, there they had done not too badly. The Greffier had taken a nice chub, and the Mayor three exceptionally fine eels, I handed up my creel, and in the rays of the carriage lamp they regarded its interior of gleaming fish and kingcups, all exclaiming and talking at once. 'What a bag, *par example*' Ah! I had given up the fly after all. Jean Pierre chuckled and climbed after me on to the back seat. So we started up the hill, a convivial party, the two in front twitting me on my good fortune with the lobworm, while I repeatedly disclaimed the use of anything but a small black fly. There was something disquieting, however, in my own reflections, for my golden stream was still a secret. No matter, this could all be explained later. We had now reached the crest of the hill, and here, on the rim of the *landes*, as if by common consent, we lapsed from monosyllables into silence, tucking our rugs more closely about our knees. The world of stillness around us was punctuated only by the rhythmic beat of the horses' hoofs as the long road slipped ever past us; but we still had many miles to go. Wise Jean Pierre had, I thought, already fallen asleep, and I settled down comfortably into my corner and pulled the rug higher across my chest.

Now we are swinging slowly downhill, the *landes* behind us, overhead the stars, only outlines are now visible. Here a crucifix looms big at a crossroads, and farther the pine tops, cut in black velvet against the night. Scent and sound are pregnant at a time like this. The smell of leaf mould; fir needles, and resin are pungent down the long avenue through which we pass. The acrid flavour of peat smoke meets us beyond. We have heard for the last mile the constant bark of a farm dog, now a turn in the road brings us to the farm. We are only aware of it by the square of light from a window. A peasant's gruff voice calls into the night and the dog ceases barking. We can hear the rattle of his chain. Figures pass silhouetted for a moment against the square of light. Then the road makes another turn, and we plunge down into further woods. From near at hand comes the sound of flowing water, an owl hoots, and is answered faintly from far away. The road leads on and on and on…

I think I must really have fallen asleep. I was roused again to consciousness by the excited accents of my friend the Mayor: *Impossible! Une mouche aujourdhui?* A whip cracked in the darkness… *Im-pos-sible!* Then came to me the voice of the Greffier: *Et vous donc! Pourquoi diable n'avions-nous pas apporté des asticots?* I was still heavy with sleep, and could not for the moment get the meaning of that last sentence. I closed my eyes again – *asticots – asticots!* What was that word? Then like a flash its meaning was recalled – Of course, maggots! The remark that the Greffier had made was: 'Why did we not, too, bring maggots?'

The Mayor looked quickly over his shoulder. 'Monsieur is still sleeping? He remarked sententiously. So Monsieur slept on as a child sleeps, smiling, till it became necessary to sit up and yawn noisily. We had passed on to the cobbles, and the horses' hoofs were waking the echoes in the village square. At the front of the inn we pulled up. The door opened, and there was Anastasie, a flickering candle held high to greet us.

No, Monsieur le Maire would not come in, as supper was awaiting himself and the Greffier. Jean Pierre should come in before taking the horse to the stable to have just one glass of cider, while helping to lay out the fish. With many goodnights we parted, and from the door I heard their voices trailing away in the darkness. Could it have been fancy that out of the night came to me again that word asticots? No, for Jean Pierre had heard it too. He chuckled as he took a pinch of snuff from his pouch. He regarded his pouch significantly, then, looking at me, he solemnly closed one eye and chuckled again.

CHAPTER II

SOME BRETON TROUT STREAMS

The interior of Brittany is cut by a long sweeping range of highlands, known locally as the Menez Arrés. If we refer to a modern large scale map we shall find this chain marked *Montagnes d'Arrée*. Yet, though dignified by the name of mountains, they are, in reality, only a succession of high moors, rock strewn, covered with gorse and heather, and nowhere do they rise to more than 1,500 feet above sea level.

With a blue pencil we can trace them on the map. Beginning at Moncontour in the east, they stretch westward, to rise parallel with St. Brieux and Guingamp. From this point they take a southwesterly direction to La Feuille, and almost as far as Le Faou. From here, again, they are marked to the south of Châteaulin and Châteauneuf and finally sink into insignificance beyond Gourin.

Our blue pencil has traced out a rough semicircle, in which lies the pick of the Breton trout fishing. In fact, this is a vast nursery for the countless brooks and streams which herein find their source. This country keeps much of its old Breton character, and can still afford good fishing to those who have the leisure and keenness to explore it for themselves. Ample time is here an essential. Brittany is not the place for the eager fisherman with only ten days at his disposal. This advice is backed strongly by an old friend's letter which now lies before me. 'Don't be the means of luring many a young man on a fool's errand, and thus make him lose a short holiday... You know' (so writes my friend) 'that even for us 'old Bretons' the fishing is hard to find and hard to get at.' Between the lines there seems to lurk a dread of our blue pencil – that it will up and mark precisely the exact length of water whereon in days gone by a dry fished palmer has accomplished much. But the map at this spot is virgin, even the little stream has been passed over unobserved. Doubtless it still is safe, and should you come to Brittany and meet my friend he'd be the first to show you his pet pool, and you would fish it while he held the landing net.

It would not here be advisable or even possible to try and direct the angler to particular pools. This is a country where poaching is rampant, and where the conditions on certain waters may change within a single season. For example, there is a small brook midway between Pont-Aven and Quimperlé which now is troutless. A few years back its fishing was excellent. It still has an occasional run of sea-trout after heavy rain. Again, there are streams in the north of Morbihan in which a few seasons ago it was not worthwhile to wet a line, but now they hold a quite respectable head of trout. Still "the fishing is hard to find and hard to get at", so justly writes my friend. The light railways which have been introduced in certain parts of Brittany have not tended to help matters. The poachers from the larger towns are thus enabled to reach some riverside by the last train out, bringing with them their nets, lanterns, and night-lines. The fish are packed before daybreak, and a few hours later are safely in an express train on their way to Paris. The local *Gardien de Pêche* is only paid fifty centimes per day by the Government for his services. Is it to be wondered at that, should he through the window see the flicker of a lantern on the riverbank, he grunts and turns over in his lit-clos, pulling his worsted nightcap securely over his ears?

In spite of all this, the fishing, on the whole, is no worse than it was ten years ago. Indeed, the census of local opinion agrees that it is better, for the Breton is becoming a keen and by no means unskilful wet fly fisher, and has, therefore, begun to look askance at the more flagrant forms of open poaching, which hitherto he condoned. Yet diffidence in narrating this fishing seems so much kinder to the reader than exaggeration. There have been articles on Breton trout fishing from time to time in our own Press which are extravagant and misleading. Such a one describes how two rods took fifty brace of trout near Châteaulin within a single day, but the writer forgets to mention that here the trout run very small, and also that the greater part of the water in the district has long since been ruined by the establishment of powder factories. No, this is not the pick of the Brittany fishing. Perhaps we can best help the fisherman by eliminating certain districts which the guide books have pointed out as being good fishing centres. Landerneau, Commana, and La Roche have been done to death by the Brest Fishing Club. Then comes the *pièce de résistance* of fishing fame. We shall find Quimperlé the most charming old town in southern Brittany if only we have enough strength of mind to keep the strings of our rod case securely fastened. This is not such an easy matter as one might suppose, for the waters of its three rivers are extraordinarily seductive to the outward eye. Only bitter experience will teach the angler that they are overfished and poached (abîmer is the local term). Quimperlé also has its fishing club.

Then there is Pont-Aven, with its delightful mill-strewn river. A few fish may be taken on the higher waters in the early spring above the third mill from the village up to the bridge at Pont, but as a whole the fishing is disappointing. That around Quimper is even worse. We have now arrived at the metropolis, where a dinner at the Épée cannot console us for spoiled waters and an empty creel. Quimper must also be eliminated as a fishing centre. In Brittany we shall come to realise that poverty and sport go hand in hand; that the farther we pass from civilisation the better will be our fishing. We shall only begin to know la vraie Bretagne when we get beyond the inroads of modern republican France and the tracks of the summer tourist. But there we shall find no well-served *table d'hôte* nor *croissants* with our early coffee.

Far in the interior of this grey land are hamlets which cannot boast a single auberge, except those at whose doors hang bunches of mistletoe. These have only one general room, and cater for the needs of thirsty peasants rather than for those of the tired fisherman. Good inns with bedrooms I was going to say – there are none. And yet I know one. Above its entrance is an ancient sign, braced fast against the wall. Its Breton lettering is spaced on a faded ground of dull gold and blue. It runs:

Inn, by permission of the King and the Parliament:
The Three Wise Men:
Dinner for foot travellers, four sols:
Lodging for foot travellers, six sols.

As my pen writes I almost feel my friend's hand plucking at my sleeve. 'For heaven's sake don't tell them that! It's more than likely that the inn is now pulled down – and...' Of course, I know; today, most probably, you can buy the signboard at Quimper. You will find it in a curiosity shop kept by a Jew. (Remember that the characters are in Breton, spaced on a ground of dull gold and faded blue.) He'll ask a thousand francs. Offer him forty: should he accept, why, then the signboard is a faked one. 'The three wise men' still stand.

We must explore the inland part of the country to find its best fishing, and the ideal way to do this is by motor. A car enables the fisherman, not only to sleep in comfort at a good hotel, but to reach easily the most remote districts where there are no inns or accommodation of any kind. If one stream proves to be dull fishing, it is always a simple matter to push on to the next. Indeed, one of the charms of this Breton fishing, is that there is always a further stream yet to explore.

At Pont-Aven the motorist will find one of the most comfortable hotels in the country. Needless to praise our old friend Mademoiselle Julia. She and her hostelry are famous throughout the length and breadth of Brittany. Again, there is the Lion d'Or at Quimperlé, Hotel Lécadre at Rochefort-en-Terre, Pontivy, with indifferent hotels, but immediately opposite the station is a restaurant with clean rooms and excellent cuisine. Quimper we know; all these are within reasonable motoring distance of good fishing. Yet a long drive after a hard day's fishing is not always an unmixed blessing, and some anglers may prefer to be on the spot, or, at any rate, within a mile or two of good water. For these there is Le Faouët. Tersely we name it, loving it too well, admitting all the poaching, all those two-pound trout braconnes, fried in butter, that you will sup off at the Croix d'Or, and fail to meet their like upon the morrow. For this is the very kernel of all illicit fishing. Yet there are still, to quote Jean Pierre, les petits endroits. Being prejudiced, perhaps, it is best to quote the guide book: "The village is situated on an eminence between the Laïta or Élle and the Ster-Laër-Inam, which afford excellent fishing. In the Place is a large covered marketplace and an avenue of elm trees. The oldest part of the town surrounds the parish church (fifteenth century). The church tower is not in the centre of the transept, but over the western facade." On a moonlight night in June the actual position seems immaterial. The looming white tower of Faouët stands dim, yet eternal, above the homes of the living and the dead. The aforementioned rivers south of the village are not worth fishing for trout, but they hold good chub, which will at times rise well to a dry fly.

The chapel of St. Fiâcre lies midway between the two

rivers. It is the most beautiful thing of its kind in all Brittany, still unrestored, mellowed by time, and containing some wonderful old stained glass and carvings. Here possibly it may be worthwhile to take a rod and walk back by way of the river. The best of the trout fishing, however, lies north and also in the Pont Rouge stream, which can be reached four miles along the old Plouay Road, and fished above the bridge. Another good centre is Huelgoat (Hotel de France) with its four rivers – the Faô, Argent, Elez, and Aulne. Close to the hotel is a lake, which in places can quite easily be fished from the bank. The best fish, however, lie where the river enters the lake. At this part are large weed beds, and a boat is necessary. The best of the river fishing is some distance from the village. The water at Brennilis is good at times.

My pen is for ever trying to run into details, to specify certain holes where once lurked big trout, and to point out bridges and weirs which have seen good sport in times gone by. Yet if we turn again to the map and our traced semicircle, we shall realise the impossibility of accurately appraising various waters. We have here before us a perfect network of watercourses and yet many of the smaller trout streams are not even indicated on the map. It is these which will provide us with the best fishing.

The larger Breton rivers are, as a rule, useless to the flyfisherman, but their tributaries can afford him good sport. The river Blavet is perhaps the one exception. It calls to mind many names, Kerbalain, Kérien, St. Nicolas-du-Pélem, and there is trout-fishing at Gauarec and as far down as Mur-de-Bretagne, and, for all I know, even farther.

We have spoken of the river Ellé. This is joined at Quimperlé by the Isole, which is also poached, and not worth fishing. The salmon fishing here is mostly in private hands.

The river Scorff is useless below Gueméne, and there are even in its upper reaches too many pike, but in spite of them the fishing is moderately good.

The flyfisherman may safely eliminate the lower waters of the Aout and Oust. The former is said to hold good trout about St. Caradec and Uzel.

Near Rochefort-en-Terre is the Arz River, which has seen dark deeds by night. Many poachers live upon its banks. Its wonderful old mills are less few and far between than its surface-feeding trout. I have often fished this beautiful river, but only once have I taken a big trout, and that my wife most skilfully landed in an umbrella.

Also there was that story, brought me by the peasants, of a giant trout who evaded poachers. He lived, this trout, far under the shade of a thick bramble patch; one never saw him, only his oily bubble. A whole afternoon I fished for him with no success, yet could not put him down. Fat bubbles forever floated out beneath the brambles in company with my unmolested fly. It was, I remember, the day of the *pardon* of St. Gravé, and the white-coiffed peasants trooped back across the plank bridge and sat in the long grass under the hawthorn trees to watch. Old Kleydan, the miller, crouched on his *sabot*s at my side. His brand new beaver hat bobbed and gesticulated wildly; in fact, his whole raiment, though doubtless it did honour to the saint's day, was quite unsuited to the riverbank. I trembled lest he should disturb those bubbles. But they continued while fly after fly was changed, given its trial beneath the bramble patch, and then discarded for another pattern. At last I rigged up on a No. 6 hook a brazen creature of tinsel, feathered with blue and scarlet. This was in sheer desperation, and yet, if the trout could stand old Kleydan's embroidered waistcoat, surely my cheerful creature would not scare him. At the second cast he had it well under water, and amidst acclamation was he landed – an ill-conditioned four-pound chub. No, the Arz is not a river for the flyfisherman, yet there are trout in some of its smaller tributaries. Moreover, upon its banks there stands a mill (perhaps the eighty-second from the sea) wherein they sell delicious sparkling cider at four sous the *litre*. You only pay three sous if you return the bottle!

This also is the country of the fearsome *Gabino* which at twilight haunts the banks of Arz. Usually it takes the form of a great black-faced goat. Should you thus meet it you will surely be driven within the river. There is only one way to avoid this. You firmly grasp your rosary, blessed by the good St. Anne, then loudly you remark: 'To hell, vile stinkard!' At these words will the *Gabino* give one low, hoarse bleat and vanish.

It is unlikely that the fisherman will meet a single trout along the River Arz, yet on its banks are often browsing goats. Curiously enough, these goats are very large, and one and all they are black-headed. A sudden face-to-face encounter in the gloaming might be, to say the least of it, confusing. The fisher on the banks of Arz should keep this tale in mind, also he must remember that the frothing cider that they sell within the eighty-second mill, at four sous the litre (you only pay three sous if you return the bottle), is wondrous potent. Above all must he not forget the magic words of imprecation. Then, if he meets a black-faced quadruped when daylight falls (no need to take unnecessary chances) he stands, he firmly grips the relic, or, failing that, the handle of his landing net; he loudly shouts: 'To hell, vile stinkard!' If nothing happens, well, then it's not the *Gabino* but only a browsing goat.

For the most part we have only touched on the larger rivers within our semicircle, but there are endless smaller streams which are well worth fishing. We shall find plenty of them from Châteauneuf-du-Faou right across to Noyal and La Vraie Croix, and here, moreover, apart from the fishing, the very beasts are said to have the power of speech. Apparently the Noyal oxen are the direct descendants of one which lived in Bethlehem at the time that the saints were arriving to prepare the manger. In fact, these good folk were somewhat perturbed at finding this great beast taking up all the room, and sore put to it to know how best to get rid of him. The old ox, however, realised the situation at once – not only was he delighted to give up his place, but he helped the saints to tidy up before he left.

At Noyal not so many years ago a drunken peasant lay in his stable sleeping while his two oxen munched their evening meal. He was awakened by the voices of his oxen as they talked. (It is Jean Pierre's, story, this, not mine.) One ox remarked: 'What shall we do tomorrow?' 'We shall bear our master to his grave,' replied the other. The drunken peasant staggered to his feet. 'You lie, cursed brute!' he screamed, raising his heavy axe. But *'vous savez,* that peasant was so very drunk and very wroth, he missed the ox and killed himself... enfin... '

If anyone should consider the dullness of writing a fishing gazetteer, he will surely condone these irrelevant deviations amongst goats and oxen. Indeed, it is an impossible task to appraise with any semblance of correct comparison these varied Breton waters. On looking back on what I have written, I realise that the desire not to say too much has led possibly to the saying of too little – to a sort of dictatorial veto on the majority of the Breton rivers. After all, as Jean Pierre says, *Il-y-a toujours des endroits* (even in the country around Quimper and Châteaulin), and these the fisherman will discover only by exploring for himself. Most of the fishing is free, and he can wander up a stream for a whole day without fear of riparian owners and their water bailiffs. He may meet occasionally a miller or a farmer. The latter cannot be compared to his brethren across the Channel, but more nearly resembles the Scotch crofter, except that he is often the owner of his small farm and soil. He is a good fellow, kindly, frugal, an indefatigable worker, and usually very poor. Yet here appearances may be deceitful. It is more than likely, although his home looks indigent and bare, that he has a pile of five-franc pieces in that old oak chest along with Madame's goffered white collars and the black-velvet dress she wears on *pardon* days.

We have spoken of the difficulty and fatigue of this fishing, and here, for the benefit of those who do not know Brittany, it is necessary to explain the character of the country. The pasturelands in the valley are cut up into countless small properties; these are not marked off simply by hedges, but by large banks crowned with gorse and stunted oak trees. High banks separate each enclosure, and prove very tiresome obstacles to the fisherman. Here waders are a necessity, not only to circumvent these hindrances, but also to reach water which is inaccessible to the local fisher. Moreover, the meadows are usually flooded in the spring, and it will be essential to wade in places in order to reach the river.

The trout season commences on February 4 and closes on September 16. Fishing after sunset is officially prohibited. The Breton regulations with regard to fishing vary slightly in the different Departments, and are placarded at the various towns and villages, where they can always be seen on the wall of the local *Mairie*, These notices are of little value, however, since the poachers and professional fishermen who supply the inns with fish are either unable or unwilling to read them.

It is as well to ask permission whenever there is any doubt as to the fishing rights on certain waters. Good manners are always worthwhile. Civility and a handshake will find a ready response in Brittany.

May I here be allowed, very tentatively, to suggest a useful phrase, which may, perhaps, be more helpful than the '*Merci, très-bien*' that the foreigner so often adopts in this country? It is this: *Je suis enchanté*. Its Breton equivalent being, *Mé a zo gwell gontant*.

Of course, we know that the average Englishman is never enchanted, and even if he were he would not like it known.

Still, this idiom pleases the Breton, so we need not take it too literally. We must also realise that we English have something to live down in Brittany. In the past our countrymen have not always been remarkable for tact or even politeness. Those of them who persist in regarding the Bretons as 'a dirty, drunken, and immoral peasantry', I would implore to keep away.

A half-truth must always sting more than falsehood, so what can we say, we who know and love the Bretons? Poverty must always lead to dirt. Let those who live on thirty sous a day disprove it. As for the charge of immorality, the whole question is preposterous. The Breton has his moral code, and we have ours. Perhaps neither is impeccable. *Nolite judicare, sine amore...* But let us render it in English as best we can. 'Do not criticise without love, without discrimination, without knowledge. None the less, I hold that a dog should always be regarded as a dog, and a pig as a pig.' Surely these animals are not indigenous in Brittany alone.

The Breton, like all idealists, is so much less happy than his dreams, yet is he fortunate because he still can dream. We must not, however, consider him merely as a visionary. He knows which side his bread is buttered, and even should there be no butter he keeps his singular sense of humour. For such a people, perhaps their negative merits can most honestly represent them. They stand in contrast with all that is Teutonic, all that is materialistic. They are not practical and are never tiresome. At seasons they are very idle. If this be a moral failing, their saints must be held responsible; and surely such drudging toil deserves its *pardon* days! They are not modernised, these Bretons. Indeed, they still put faith far before scientific fact; and should they meet and understand the most recent of philosophising pedants he would leave them cold. They are wiser, for they have learned that life is never demonstrable, that two and two do not of necessity make four.

These people, moreover, do not yet enjoy the advantages of the modern newspaper. There are still districts which have never felt the iron hand of a syndicated Press.

For many years the beggars were the only recognised bearers of official news. Even today they hold an honoured place at fireside and board. The Breton beggar was also the purveyor of the *guerz*, or national ballads, which were sung throughout the country; also of the *sônes*, or admonitory songs, which were composed by and for the peasantry. The most typical of these is 'The Cholera Song,' which was composed during the epidemic somewhere about 1867. The priests had placards printed and pasted up on the graveyard walls and doors of each village. These notices bore the stamp of authority. They explained at some length what the people ought and what they ought not to do to avoid the cholera. All water must be flavoured with vinegar. No fruit must be eaten, and so on and so forth. The Bretons did not see them! Even those who could read realised that printed matter was a dangerous thing, not to be meddled with, least of all to be looked at. They tilted their broad-brimmed hats over their eyes and passed by on the other side. Then fortunately the priesthood bethought them of a better plan. They sent for the local maker of *sônes*, and he pared down their printed placard into a couple of verses, and set them to a well-known tune. Within the week this warning had reached the most lonely and out-of-the-way farmhouses. The beggars sang 'The Cholera Song' from end to end of Brittany.

The *guerz* is fast dying out in this land, but the beggars still carry the *sônes* today. Should a latter-day Breton poet become a dry fly enthusiast, he will strike terror to the hearts of the people. We shall have the *sône of the poacher*, and Brittany will become an angling paradise.

The Breton is *bugel-fur* (a wise child). So wise and childlike is he, that his priests have been hard put to it how best to manage him. For untold ages he worshipped the sun. During the summer solstice a thousand fires blazed on the Breton *landes*. Today these fires still flame, but the priests have discreetly blessed them; the roaring faggots of the Thunder God are now kindled to the honour of St. John. Oh, but this Eve of St. John is wonderful! Stand on a hillside in Morbihan as this night of June begins to wrap the lower *landes* in mystery – watch as a single fire starts into flame. As the night darkens, flickering points of light spring up along the *landes*. They grow and widen to the distant skyline. A red glare fills the earth. A thousand sacred fires are blazing.

Listen, you will hear a sonorous whisper rising and falling with the breeze. The murmured melody grows clearer. Such exultation for the good *Saint Jean*! But now the chant is harsher. It seems to press, to dwell upon one pagan note. Surely the ancient gods have wakened and walk the *landes* tonight!

Listen again – through the wild chant floats another sound, unearthly, obscure, booming on the air – the sacred rites have reached that part which is called *the milking of the goat*.

Let us come down and see. The path is steep and rugged, yet should we stumble in the dark it is not unlikely that Pan, goat-footed, will lend a kindly hand and lead us to the fires. We reach the first. There in the flickering light the old folks are praying. They pick at their strings of beads. They mutter. Then from the shadows plunge two comely girls, dishevelled now and fighting madly, all for one scorched and faded flower. The rose that crowned the bonfire is a wondrous talisman; worn on a woollen yarn against a maiden bosom, it brings complete happiness in love. Why, even a charred twig snatched from the holy fire can protect from thunder.

The chant rolls on, while in the waves of glowing light the swaying figures circle.

Again there comes that weird booming on the air. It grows, it vibrates, numbing all other sounds. Pan leads us through the throng, which parts asunder; we reach two kneeling figures. Low they bend over a vast brazen pan. They hold wet green rushes taut from rim to rim. Between them kneels a third, who slowly draws the reeds between his fingers with a motion as of milking. At his touch they answer vocally. They sob and shudder in the darkness. Then with an iron key he strikes them. They cry aloud. The sound vibrates and pulses in the air. Only if your name is Jean may you perform this ritual. My friend Jean Pierre... But let us come down the valley to a second fire, and join the merry party round the blaze. The girls are dancing still. Here a youthful *Saint Jean* officiates. This chubby saint who tweaks the rushes is but four years old. His mother's restraining hand holds fast the seat of his small trousers, while the saint plays on in tune with happy laughter.

At the lonely farm of Kestrec a third fire smoulders. An hour ago it roared and blazed, but now the night grows late. One by one the peasants have crept away, leaving the dying embers to the spirits of the dead. The foremost has arrived already, for old Jean Gratien is more a spectre than a living man, so ancient and beyond his time is he. He crouches low, his listless hands lie still upon the bowl of brass. The reeds are silent, only the white lips move. This is no Catholic canticle we hear, but a barbaric dirge, mouthed in Old Breton, an unknown tongue we may not understand, and yet the eyes are speaking. They grow older than the cromlech stones. They gaze beyond us, seeing the whole travail of the world. They peer into deep waters where the hopes of men lie dead. They reach all gladness and all pain, even to those depths which shroud all things unutterable. Their lids are seamed with sorrow and with tears.

Is it a trick of fancy that old Gratien is transformed? His clothes have bleached, and hang from his lean shoulders in spacious folds. His head is raised. We mark its leafy chaplet. The ancient Breton listens.

Soft and thin and far away there steals a cadence on the

ear. It grows, resounds along the *landes*. Clear are the voices through the oak wood glades; sonorous they echo down the valley-way to rise in thunder beside the granite stones, and fall again in mute expectancy. The silence deepens, touched only by clean swish of sickle through the mistletoe, the crackling of the sacred fire, the thud of sacrifice upon the altar stone – the gods have answered.

Of course, to the sound Church of England mind all this is rank idolatry. A trait contemptible displaying the ignorance of the peasantry. Perhaps – God knows; until we know, let's leave it. You say the Breton drinks – yes, terribly at times, because – and there is no incongruity in this – because he is an idealist. He sees visions which he cannot reach. He dreams dreams, which never come true. Is it for nothing that he still can use the ancient Breton prayer: 'Saints ivrognes de Bretagne, priez pour nous'? Liquor stupefies him, but cannot make him brutal or vindictive. He may lie helpless in a ditch, and yet he always sees the stars.

Perhaps we love him most because he has escaped orthodoxy. He clings to the fringe of immortality. His land is still fey. Along his moors are *menhir*s, each crowned with a cross of stone. He worships both the *menhir* and the cross.

We have irrelevantly wandered so far beyond the Breton streams that one turn further brings us to the land of legend.

It happened in the days of the Deluge, that St. Peter and St. Paul were travelling the world to see what was a-doing, and they reached the land of Brittany in the height of the rain and the wind. The two poor saints were drenched to the skin, besides being cold and hungry, and though they knocked loudly at many doors, they could not make themselves heard, so great was the roaring of the tempest.

At length they reached the hovel of one called *Misery*, and this they entered, for the door was broken. Old Gaffer *Misery* was crouching by the empty hearth, but when he saw the two bedraggled wayfarers he staggered to his feet, murmuring words of welcome. 'Sit down, good friends,' said he, 'the while I light these bits of charred driftwood to give us warmth and dry your clothing.' The two saints sat in the firelight, while the old man busied himself about their needs. Going at length to a broken cupboard, from which he took his sole store of food, some few crusts of black bread, these he laid before the strangers. .

When the charred wood had burnt out and the bread was all eaten, St. Peter said to *Misery*: 'Thou art a good man; thou hast given us all. Thy charity is real, for it was given for the love of God. May thy faith equal thy charity. Ask what thou most desirest. It shall be granted thee'. At these words *Misery* realised that he was in the presence of the saints. He fell on his knees before them. 'Oh, most holy ones!' he said, 'I have but a single possession, and that is an apple tree – one little apple tree – yet every year am I robbed of its fruit while I am gone a-begging. Grant me, therefore, that whosoever shall climb my apple tree shall have no power to descend from its branches without my leave'. With bowed head he knelt upon the earthen floor and waited till the answer came. 'Thy wish is granted;' but when he looked up and gazed around him, behold, he was alone, the place was empty.

Only the storm stayed on with *Misery*, who crouched by the cold hearth gazing at its white ashes and listening to the ceaseless drip, drip of the rain from the cracked and broken roof. Ever and again did he totter painfully to the cupboard in the wall, only to find it empty; not a crumb of his sour bread remained. Three days and nights did the tempest rage, but the fourth dawn broke with an aisle of tender light across the *landes*. It glistened on the wet leaves of the apple tree, and even faintly tinged an old lined face that nodded above the gloomy hearthstone.

Then was the light shadowed for a moment. The old man slowly opened his eyes, craning to recognise a dark, still figure that stood within the doorway. Another traveller had come to the house of *Misery.*

The stranger's voice was harsh. 'Your time has come, *Misery.* Are you ready? Are you ready now to follow me?'

'My good friend,' said the old man, 'you should know that I am always ready, for I have nothing to take out of the world and nothing to leave in it; and yet before I go hence even I have one lingering wish – I would eat once of the fruit of my apple tree. Surely you who are so kind cannot refuse me this!'

The stranger laughed. 'Oh, *Misery*' he said, 'there are others who have asked a greater thing than this – one cider apple! – and here it lies amidst the clustered apples in the grass. The storm has stripped the fruit from your frail apple-tree.'

Then *Misery* with a trembling finger pointed. 'Pity', he said, 'an old man's last request. The storm has left one single apple still unbruised upon the topmost branch.'

The stranger laughed again. 'If that is all,' he said, 'one small crabbed apple.'

He swung into the tree, but there he stayed, moving in impotence among the branches, bound by a power greater than his own. He strove to break the tree, but could not. He raved, he struggled, all in vain.

Then said Death to *Misery*, 'If you will let me go, I have so much to do, I swear to give you ten long years.' But *Misery* snarled through his paucity of teeth: 'Ten years forsooth! I wait for the coming of God and judgment!' Then Death howled among the leaves. He gibbered like an ape, shaking the branches, while *Misery* mocked from below. At length Death panted, 'Have your own way,' he gasped; 'you shall live on to the end of all things.'

So was Death freed, and sprang from the apple tree, gripping his scythe. In rage he passed on through the *landes* slaying the old folk and the children as well.

There is one only whom he may never touch – *Misery* dwells on through eternity – waiting the Judgment Day.

CHAPTER III

RANDOM MEMORIES

I have here before me a pocket edition of *The Compleat Angler*. Its binding is somewhat worn, and has mellowed to a wonderful colour. Its date is 1826. This little volume provides much food for reflection, even before we turn the flyleaf. We may possibly know its minute and careful instructions in the art of angling, but I think the chief reason why this book is read and reread and will never be forgotten is because Walton loved fishing. Poor old Piscator, what delight he had in those days spent by the riverside, and yet, should he return and join his brother anglers on those same banks today, what an affair! Can't we see him perplexedly fingering the oil bottle, and imagine his expression of wonder at the modern ginger-quill tied on a down-eyed No. 00. But just listen to the fellow: 'You have length enough; stand a little further off, let me entreat you, and do but fish the stream like an artist, and peradventure, a good fish may fall to your share'. Isn't he wonderful? A whole treatise on the art of casting and all perfectly condensed into three lines.

Who with such a fascinating mentor at his side could venture to discourse on rods and lines and tackles, or attempt the exact precepts of the angler's lore? No; our only hope is to be frankly irrelevant, just to talk of the days and the pleasures we have loved, so perchance we may stir kindred memories, and others may be able to slip into a corner of our mood and share with us some of the delight of happy moments.

Oh, if this were only easy! But the nature of a fisherman's joy is a subtle quality. It cannot be adequately expressed in written characters, nor is it occasioned by the mere catching of fish. Birds come into it, and flowers and the spring sunshine, and there is nature-magic, too, which even winged words would fail to touch. If, therefore, we may share only a little of our joy with brothers of the blood, what fragment of its fringe will others find – our other friends who do not fish? 'But isn't it rather dull?' They ask, remembering Paris, and vaguely a long line of fishers, motionless and vigilant, who guard the river Seine. 'It would require too much patience'. For them it would, and doubtless we are wise to keep a golden silence, thankful for waters yet not over-fished, and friends who still respect a patient, meditative turn of mind, even when they find us odd and very dull. Perhaps, however, that philosophic and contemplative mood which is necessary to perfect contentment in angling only comes with years. Youth is so full of the fever of pursuit that there is no time to put the rod down even for five minutes while we light a ruminative pipe. Unfortunately, some of us never grow up. We are too keen on excitement. We change our fly often, and rush on from pool to pool, harassed and worried, spoiling what should be the joy of a summer's day. Yet none of us can quite spoil it. Sooner or later we begin to realise a sense of freedom, of mental detachment. We find emotional elbowroom – time to think, to rediscover the things in life which really count. Mother Earth is very near in those hours by the waterside, that are so long and golden.

It was not for nothing that a canon law of the ancient Church prescribed fishing for the clergy as being 'favourable to the health of their body, and specially of their soules.'

Jean Pierre will have it that all good fishermen are good fellows, and that no really bad man ever cares for fishing: *Et vous savez il font avoir foi dans la pêche, car la foi est un don du bon Dieu.* Apparently the one exception to the rule is the miller of Kerval. But, then, Jean maintains that the miller is no fisherman.

With all this elevated matter in mind, it were, perhaps, as well to turn for a while to the more material aspect of a fisherman's experience, recalling the sheer joy of successfully landing a big fish on fine gut and with an eight-ounce rod; also that unregenerate moment when an even greater trout lies under the shadow of a may tree sucking down flies, while our own is fixed firmly in the lowest branch a foot above his neb. If only we dared to break off that fly. The slightest pull on the line is certain to scare the fish and put him down, but it is our last resort. We try it, snapping the cast just as the fish turns after his rise. He has not seen us. He is still feeding! On all fours we creep back to the safety of the long grass. Hurriedly we adjust a fresh fly, while every nerve is strung, our fingers trembling. Surely there is something primitive and pagan about all this, yet it is delightful all the same.

Then, too, there is that sensuous and very human feeling which possesses a man after a long day's fishing. He has dined. He is very tired, but he still retains an extraordinary consciousness of wellbeing. His slippered feet are warmed by a generous wood fire, and he remembers! No need to fetch that gleaming dish of fish reposing in the dim coolness of the larder. He has them all. That big trout in rough water nearly weeded him, and this plump fellow of the withy-bed. What bungling had been there! That was a case of nerves; nerves, slack line, and luck. It is not by heavy bags alone that we count happy days at the riverside. There are many minor incidents, trifling in themselves, which, when bunched together one by one, will bloom again in fragrant retrospect.

Yet we found no flavour in that moment when we moved a step too far, flooding our waders, cut an inch too short. Nor in those weary hours when we trudged home belated, nor in those tangled thickets, trackless wastes, through which we crawled, torn, tired, hungry, in the dark. Strange that the poignancy of such distress can pass, to leave only the keen savour of fried eggs at suppertime. As for those waders, their chill clamminess is gone; while our wood fire crackles we keep only the sweet warm sent of clover buds, the ripple of the river as it passed a great flat stone, a yellow bush of gorse, whereon inverted waders hang, steaming in hot sunshine...

It's early yet. Our fire still burns red, and in its glow there lies a well-remembered valley, where the asphodel only a few short weeks ago broke in a mist of cream and rose. Now wild forget-me-not grows down to the edge of the peat-coloured water, interspersed with the young green shoots of butterwort.

There are tussocks of coarse grass beyond the yellow gravel spit, where a sandpiper has her nest. She flutters off, but watches anxiously, close at hand, feigning a broken wing, till a rising fish in the pool above draws us from her zone of danger. The eggs will be hatched within the next few days.

This upper stretch of stream is long and straight. Its gurgling headwaters are fairly shallow, making a ford for cattle, and spanned by a low bridge of giant stones, where a single stunted pine keeps sentinel. Here the current chuckles and gurgles past high banks of heather, and then lies deep and grows quiet, just murmuring as it eddies past some lichen-covered boulders. Each rock forms an oily glide, which is broken now and again by a widening circle. This can be an eerie spot after sundown, when curlews call across the marshes and the mists begin to rise. Now our thoughts lead on, tracing down the riverbank to a spot where the moor begins to merge with pastureland. We reach this pool by a path through a tangled thicket where white foxgloves grow. A broad reach this, needing a long cast and a stiff and powerful rod. It starts off with an amber stickle, water about two foot deep, full, too, of good trout when they are on the feed. Jean Pierre calls this pool le dernier sou. It is, in fact, the gambler's last throw, and if fish cannot be induced to take a fly here, then the chances of sport are hopeless.

Further down this pool is fringed with whin bushes, so placed that a feeding fish may be taken at each intervening space. Every trout fights desperately for the shelter of his own particular bush, and, even though well hooked, is not necessarily landed. But the cream of this water lies under its far bank, where live some really big fish, who may be induced in a fading light to suck down a well placed alder. Further again in the still depths dwells the Leviathan. Rumour has it that once, on a dark and starless night, was Leviathan led astray by an ample and elderly grasshopper. But the latter's known preference for sunshine and early habits makes us doubt the story. Jean Pierre suspects a cockroach, and his experiences with cockroaches on dark nights are not to be despised. Yet the point can never be settled, because Leviathan, so 'tis said, snapped a length of salmon gut around that post which marks the entrance to the millrace. Yes, there is a mill beyond the next bend, and everyone who has fished on Breton streams will recognise this particular pool, will even hear again the constant cracking of the gorse pods in the noonday heat. Indeed, there are scores of such pools in Lower Brittany, each with its watermill, and to these is the angler indebted for the general preservation of the trout. The stored waters above each milldam are usually deep and extensive, and to them the fish descend in hot, dry weather. They are so full of snags and holes that they cannot easily be poached with a net, and so a good breeding stock is thus maintained. Alas! The net is not alone responsible for the depletion of some of our Breton rivers. There are other methods of destruction, such as the use of lime and even dynamite.

There will be times when the angler will need all his self-control to preserve outward appearances, bitter times when, if he can keep silence, he shall keep his soul. The mental attitude of the philosopher is difficult of attainment. That

miraculous hatch of olive duns is apt to lose some of its
charm on a fishless length of stream, and it is no easy matter
to study botany round the margin of a pool that was scoured
overnight by a drag net.

Let us pass on to happier thoughts of small red worms.
These are regarded with passion by the Breton trout during
the hot summer months. If here the chalk stream exquisite
should rise up in contemptuous anger we take no offence.
We are too cosy by the fire even to argue. Besides, he does
not know Jean Pierre, and to fish the small red worm as
does Jean Pierre is a consummate art. He seems to esteem
it most in bright, hot weather, when the water is at its lowest
and crystal clear. It is a joy to watch our old friend stalking
cautiously upstream, working his way like an otter, his great
gaunt figure always under cover of a boulder or some patch
of brushwood. Then that delightful underhand cast of his,
which appears ever to be flicking the bait into a clump of
thistles or a rosebush on the opposite bank, but always sets it
lightly just where it should, to slip into the current and work
naturally with no drag. And here, be it noted, there is never
a moment of slack line. The line coils itself automatically on
skilled fingers, so if a trout should follow down and grab the
worm at Jean Pierre's feet the strike comes instantly. He gets
short shrift, this trout, no leisure to explore the overhanging
banks for roots or other entanglements. Jean Pierre does not
believe in tender tactics. I have never seen him lose a fish
for want of dexterity or reasonable care, yet were he a 'dry
fly man' he would break the heart of more than one of our
ultra-delicate rods within a season. Yet is not the quality of
decided force necessary to success in fishing? So much has
been written on the 'gentle art', that the novice has been led
to believe quite naturally that irresolute tenderness will help
him to catch fish, whereas your really fine fisherman is never
finicking or uncertain. That well-cocked fly which has fallen
perfectly was attained by no half-hearted methods, but is the

outcome of a direct and powerful cast with plenty of muscle behind it. Again, the pull home in the strike of a rising fish may be a subtle inspiration, but is certainly not a tentative wobble.

Only on a brook of fair size does Jean Pierre ply his upstream methods. On the smaller waters we fish down, or any way that fancy leads us. The Breton *landes* contain numbers of these narrow runnels, so small that it would seem impossible that they should hold such plump and sparkling trout. They are always the excuse, should one be needed, for a walk through this wonderful country of charm, and they can supply us with a good dish of fish to carry home in the evening.

Whatever our friend of the chalkstream may have to say in disparagement of worm fishing, we would answer: 'Come with us, and watch Jean Pierre'. Surely this fishing has a tempting variety, a change of methods. It is pleasant to see our line travelling down between overhanging banks in the rushing current. Suddenly the line stops. We feel that slight but unmistakable tremor that electrifies our rod-point, and passes on to our hand for the moment before we strike. A trout is actually in negotiation with our small red worm. Can we but strike in that fraction of time between the 'too soon' and the 'too late', the fish is hooked. But in this water and on such fine tackle the capture of even a well-hooked fish is by no means a foregone conclusion. He may dash up or down stream and entangle the cast in a dozen traps along the bank. In any case he will fight furiously, splashing in peril on the surface; only is he ours when he lies well back from the streamlet's brim on his terse grown heather bed.

Perhaps the most brilliant of Jean Pierre's achievements at the brook side is dapping. For this purpose he uses a short stiff rod. Above his cast he ties a small grass bent, so that the line may not slip back through the rod rings. Below this grass check hangs three feet of straight fine cast, tipped by a very small hook, which impales a dead 'bluebottle'. On this adventure he always carries with him a stout pair of clippers, which are very necessary in cutting or enlarging holes in the brushwood through which he may insert his rod. One specially remembered stream is so overgrown with thorn and whin bushes that no artificial fly has ever touched its waters, and there is hardly a gap through which a worm could find its way. This Jean Pierre loves above all others. I see him now cunningly thrusting his rod through a carved cave of branches, then gently lowering the point till the deceased bluebottle rests on the surface of the water. It is great fun, too, to be in the soft grass at the edge of the bank and watch, for Jean Pierre has become a wizard. He is now rhythmically tapping his rod-butt, and one expects that at any minute he may break into an incantation, some Breton equivalent of that *Abracadabra* that thrilled us in the golden days of picture books. But he only keeps on tapping, while through the leafy screen of twigs the dead bluebottle is seen to be keeping even time, for ever dancing on the face of the waters.

This continues endlessly, till unexpectedly there is a movement in the murky depths and a dark fin shows for a moment on the surface, but some distance away from the bluebottle, who is now footing it famously, while Jean Pierre makes the time. Then comes a second splash in the water a good two feet nearer the fly, who is now dancing furiously, while our old friend's mouth grows tight, and curiously tremulous lines appear at its corners. Then, on a sudden, his rod bends. There is a short, sharp fight, till a net is dexterously inserted in a lower cave, previously cut, close above the bank (Jean Pierre takes no unnecessary chances). Through this opening a fat pound trout emerges and is plumped upon the grass. Surely Jean Pierre is a wizard, for on most summer days he can thus account for five good brace at least!

Should you and I essay his methods, not only might we lose

a brace of fish, but also we might fail to keep our tempers. Once we get talking of our friend Jean Pierre we are led on to so many river happenings, that, could we picture but a half of them, we'd never bank the fire and get to bed. Yet one of them is clearer than all the rest, wherein Jean Pierre girds up his bragou-bras to wade the reeded stream. It happened on a day in May, perfect beyond recount, only I know all things went right, the sun shone and no single fish came short. By late afternoon we had reached, with heavy bag, the lower waters of Kerval. Good fishing this, but difficult, for tall dry beds of reed grow in the peat soil to the water's edge. The land is boggy and vibrates under a careless foot. One must walk circumspectly or scare the fish. On that day nothing could go wrong. My last brace were two beauties. Jean Pierre netted them, and curiously enough these fish had each a length of fine string protruding from his jaws.

It was then that I felt Jean Pierre's hand upon my arm. We backed together to the shelter of high reeds and watched, while round the river bend came a dilapidated punt, poled by an ancient Charon. In answer to my whispered query came the low sibilant reply: *C'est le vieux meunier – le salaud!* We crouched, and marked the miller of Kerval driving tall wooden stakes into the sand along the riverbed. The whole thing lasted but a minute, then the punt turned and drifted down between the ranks of whispering reeds, while Jean Pierre hip deep waded through the current. In turn he reached each quivering stake pole and heaved it out on to the bank. So were all twelve retrieved, each with its two-foot length of string, its giant hook, its small suspended stickleback. One by one the strings were safely cut. The poles were broken. Then did Jean Pierre retire to sit upon the hillside and dry his nether garments in the last of the evening sunlight. There I soon joined him, sitting down in the long grass to light a pipe. 'If that old scoundrel must practise his beastly tricks,' I said, 'why doesn't he fix his poles below the mills, where surely the water is better suited to his purpose?' Jean Pierre chuckled. 'Ah! He knows only too well where lie the pink-fleshed trout; below the mill are big fish, but white fleshed, poor for eating. The further you go, the more lean and pallid do those fish become. Then monsieur does not know that desolate country down by the sea – no hedges, no flowers, just a treeless tract, where no birds sing?' Jean Pierre was fumbling for his snuff pouch, a sure sign of reminiscent anecdote. I lay still in the long grass and listened...

'They say that many years ago this land was stolen from the sea. A rich farmer stole it, not a Breton, but a foreigner, who came to these parts boasting that he would reclaim the soil. The peasants would not help him build his dyke, for they said: "That which is stolen does not profit a man, and least of all that which is stolen from the sea. The sea lends us this land for eight hours each day, when we come to the beach with our carts to bring home the seaweed. Now you tell us we may no longer come, even the little corners of bitter grass you have taken from our sheep." But the rich farmer only laughed, calling them ignorant and foolish. He sent for other workmen, who came all the way from Vannes. So they laboured at his dyke of stone to bar the way of the sea. But the sea broke it at the next spring tides; after that came the priest to reason with him, to point out the people's ancient rights, their poverty, their need of seaweed to manure their fields. But the rich man made reply: "I care not for the people." Then said the priest: "I come not from the people, but from God. Monsieur, God does not sell his property." The rich man's only answer was a blasphemy. So the priest turned and retraced his steps swiftly through those stolen lands, where the first blades were showing green along the furrows, filled with salt seawater.

Then came a day when the dyke was completed. The golden corn lay thick on all the land. The rich man sat content within his solid house of granite. Yet was he ever conscious of a small dark cloud that, like some hovering hawk, poised in the west before his open window. Then came a time when all the land grew still. The cloud loomed nearer till it darkened the whole earth, while the waves of the sea broke fiercely against the dyke, bursting in clouds of spray. The waves rose higher and higher, till with a roar the dyke crumbled, and the sea entered quickly to surround his house. But he escaped it, flying inland; only at the pool of Kerval did it catch him, where he was hurled screaming into murky depths... The peasants say that during the spring tides a dead white face still faintly gleams beneath the waters of Kerval. They all agree, moreover, that the trout of this region are white fleshed, tasteless and insipid. *On dit ça, mais...*' Jean Pierre shrugged, smiling back at me. He always concludes his most preposterous tales with this remark. As that consoling *mais* was drawled, he slipped the last of those twelve sticklebacks into one horny palm and rose apologetically, murmuring something about stretching his stiff legs, and thus he hurried off.

Jean Pierre at times is like a spoiled child. I knew just where he'd gone, to lay those twelve small sticklebacks upon the miller's doorstep. The beginning of that ancient feud is wrapt in mystery. There is a rumour concerning a brace of partridges which were left one night for safety's sake within the ruined chapel of St. Sezny and vanished before morning. Another tells of a gory fight above the corpse of a great illicitly captured salmon. The latter story Jean Pierre stoutly denies, explaining that the miller in the darkness slipped and fell into the river. I think the real reason of Jean Pierre's dislike is that the miller is close-fisted. In fact, he is known among his tenants as *Grippe-sou*, and Jean Pierre hates a miser as he hates the devil. My old friend has his faults. Indeed, at seasons I have known him very, very drunk, but never once mean or ungenerous. He cannot understand the hoarder's point of view. 'To save for our old age would be but to collect nuts for when we shall have no teeth left to crack them'. Not only in this respect does his outlook differ from that of the ordinary peasant. On the morning of bleak reality after a night's potations there are no maudlin whinings; no extenuating circumstances can plead for Jean Pierre. He sits in hard-eyed realisation of fact, his head unbowed. Surely at such a time his patron saint has pity and forgives! Fortunately, these mornings are rare, and the remainder find him, his old gun slung from his shoulder, singing as he brushes through the gorse on the hillside; or perhaps we shall discover him down by the river, his long rod laid aside, while in company with two small white-coiffed children from the farm he gropes for crayfish amongst the boulders. He will turn with that whimsical smile of his. 'Ah; monsieur! Late on such a morning, and such a time as we have had too, a whole mine of treasures! Six *clochettes* have we found, and placed them in the fairy ring for the *poulpiquets** when they come to dance tonight. Little Mariic here has touched God's brightest golden feather (Jean Pierre always calls butterflies 'God's feathers') before it flew away, and Suzanne's mother will make a good crayfish stew for supper.'

Of course all children adore Jean Pierre. He is a great big child himself, a charming companion by the riverside. His knowledge of the ways of fish is only surpassed by his lore in Breton legend, and yet I think the cloak of superstition rests lightly on the shoulders of Jean Pierre. One can almost catch the covert wink at the conclusion of the dire history of *Mary Morgan*, 'who still combs her green hair midst the reeds by the pool in the first faint blush of a summer morning.' Again, on cold winter nights, when the wind whistles at the fast-closed door, and the peasants in the farm kitchen draw

* The *poulpiquets* are the husbands of the fairies. They may still be seen on moonlight nights in remote parts of Brittany where the tourist has never penetrated.

closer round the fire, none may then compete in rhetoric with Jean Pierre.

He knows every detail of the doings of the *Loup-garou*, and the very words muttered by the *Ankou* as he drives his death cart down the *Chemin Creux*. But should the wind grow higher, wakening the children, making them climb from their warm beds to stand, barefooted, round-eyed, in the firelight, then would Jean Pierre cut short his eloquence, hold out his arms and smile. *On dit ça, mais…* a shrug, the little ones are drawn to his knees and comforted. Yet must not Mariic sit upon that little stool within the chimney place, that little stool which still stands vacant by many a peasant hearth in unknown Brittany, a sort of sanctuary for the penates, sacred to the ancestral dead. 'Ah, no!' Jean Pierre insists, 'to nudge your betters off the edge to sit among the embers, and you a great fat girl, too! You see it would be uncomfortable for them. Your *grand'tante* suffered from excessive corpulence, and always needed space.'

Then memory pictures Mariic snuggled at my old friend's feet, toasting her toes before the fire, eyeing him quizzically as children will, searching his impenetrable face, his set mouth, where crinkling corners almost tremble. As his smile breaks it mingles with her own…

In some such daydream Jean found me on the hillside. He spoke no word, but ever and anon his thoughts plucked at the corners of his mouth. We packed our rods in silence, and with the last of the twilight started off up the steep track to the open *landes* above. Here the first evening star was shining, reflected in a moorland tarn, and far away on the sky-line loomed the long, low farmstead of Sezny. Why this lonely pile of ancient stone should have been given the name of a Breton saint even Jean Pierre could not tell, but he gave me the saint's whole history as we tramped home across the moors. It seems that this St. Sezny – or should we call him 'Mr.' or 'Brother', as he only becomes a saint later in the story

– was one of the first men who came from Ireland to preach the 'true faith' to the Bretons. On the very first night of his arrival he seems to have fallen out with the rich farmer of the district, who refused to give him a night's lodging. Nothing daunted, Brother Sezny starts out to build a *chapel* for shelter, and runs the whole thing up in a few hours… 'For the stones came unaided and placed themselves in their proper places, like sheep when they enter the fold at nightfall'. Jean Pierre has at times the poet's vision. His description of the fate of the rich farmer was vivid, if less ethereal; but the story has its climax some years later. St. Sezny is standing alone on the moorlands, when he hears the voice of God the Father saying unto him: 'Saint Sezny, I have just made thee a saint. From this moment thou belongest to the heavenly host. Henceforth thou shalt be the patron of women.'

'Mon Seigneur,' replies the Saint, trembling, 'if it is of Thy good pleasure to hear the prayers of poor sinners, I would entreat to be excused from so hard a task, and allowed to be the patron of tailors or shoemakers.'

'Well, then,' said the Almighty, 'since thou art so delicate, I will advance thee a grade: thou shalt be the patron of sick dogs.' *'Oh, c'est vrai!'* Jean Pierre added – *'c'est vrai!'* and, you see, St. Sezny was delighted. He was a very good saint, but not stouthearted. He was not what you would name a bold man, and he became a saint late in life; perhaps he had had some experience. We were now passing the entrance to the farm of Sezny, and a dog howled in the darkness. Jean Pierre chuckled. *'Oui, c'est vrai;* and ever since that day, you see, the dogs of Brittany have had a patron saint… '

Then softly spake Jean Pierre beneath the silent stars: 'Women,' he said, 'are wonderful, better and purer and truer than we men; and there are times, monsieur, when I see lovers walking in the lanes, their little fingers locked, or when the children call to me as they come back from school. Then at these times would I curse that simpleton Jean

Pierre, the man who never knew his mind, save that I see all the pauvre ivrogne has missed, and pity him. To have found one's woman – to be sure – that was a marvel. But *figurez-vous*, monsieur, I have never been sure, never of one single thing in all my life' …Jean Pierre spoke bitterly.

'And even that's not true, for when I'm drunkest, deep in my black heart, I know, I'm sure, that I'll be drunk again'.

For a long time we walked in silence, till Jean Pierre's sudden chuckle made me start. 'Monsieur will know the widow Floric? The well-rounded little woman with sloe-like eyes, who keeps the tobacco shop upon the *place. Vous savez*, all the village folk are matchmakers. They tell me she is an angel of patience. So she may be, but an angel who cannot endure contradiction. No, no; the old boat that has weathered so many storms unaided had best find port alone… and who am I to say that good Saint Sezny was a fool?'

CHAPTER IV

JEAN PIERRE AND THE MAYFLIES

It has been often a matter of contention whether the first morning pipe be the sweeter, or that which we draw on contentedly after the cloth has been cleared away, our glasses filled, and the final turf placed on the glowing peats. A great deal can be said for that last pipe, which, before a dreamless sleep, soothes tired and contented muscles. Perhaps its fragrance is only made complete when we have said goodnight, climbed up to our room, thrown open the persiennes, and leant on the window bar above the sleeping village. All below us is still and silent. The white houses in the little square are luminous, a-shimmer – our pipe burns faint and grey against the twinkling stars.

Jean Pierre and I have often discussed the merits of tobacco (my old friend does not use it in ignited form, but keeps an open mind), yet possibly our conception of this word is ultra delicate, for when we say *tabac* we do not mean cigars. To us the pipe seems sound, a very honest fellow. The cigarette may be more finikin and perchance less moral, still its inhalation bespeaks the true lover of tobacco. It shows an unfeigned, ring-wreathed satisfaction. True the cigar can puff a smug blue round, but one that partakes only of vainglory, and seems to fail in real affection. You know the pose of most cigars, their lack of modesty and all the finer feelings. Their air of protruding ostentation between the teeth, provocative, presumptuous? Of course, all this is quite unreasonable. We can only take refuge in a saying of Jean

Pierre's. 'Cigars,' says he, 'are not for true lovers of tobacco. They are only for *milords* and *commis-voyageurs*, who sometimes fish and always play the fool. Besides, cigars are an extravagance. In Brittany they cost, at least, two sous, and smell like nothing that the *Bon Dieu* made'. And here, to save my friend, I must explain. The word *milord* figures constantly in Jean Pierre's discourse, but has no reference to our esteemed aristocracy. It simply means an Anglo-Saxon tourist who comes to Brittany and will not understand. No, not the language, but the things that count.

Concerning pipes and talking of tobacco, we would not slight their vesper fragrance. Yet surely, for all of us, the after breakfast pipe must touch the more perfect flavour. It comes to us virginal, fresh at the youth of day, holding all promise, 'the worldly hope men set their hearts upon', before it turns to ashes. For the toilers of the city it must be fraught with a wealth of reminiscence, suggestions of holidays, halcyon days, and loafing home-spuns, of sunny lawns, of breakfasts served beneath the trees, clotted-cream, and ample honey – freedom, no early train to catch. For a time they shall escape the fetters of their offices, the sounds of commerce, clerks, and squeaking pens. Awhile they shall listen with ear attuned to fairy voices a-tinkle in the sun-drenched copse or along the dewy hedgerow.

If these be the simple joys of the lay mind, then for the initiate in angler's lore the matutinal oblation must hold a deeper, sweeter savour. This is the hour when, pipe alight, we dawdle, selecting flies and soaking casts, adding a fine drawn point. Eternal hope sits at our side whispering of ways to circumvent a certain lusty trout located overnight just at the corner of the withy-bed.

For me no pipe has tasted half so sweet since that morning of early June when Jean Pierre and I went fishing. On such a day you smoke it only as far as you must tread the dusty high road; like to the faithful who loose their shoes from off their feet when entering holy ground, so you knock out the dottle on the last kilometre stone and then turn off into Pan's sun-splashed temple.

We took the *chemin creux*, a leafy way cut between high hedgerows heavy with the scent of honeysuckle. A tunnel of green and gold, so deep that its dew does not dry till noon, but above the sun caught a wild rose spray where a yellowhammer hung for a moment, and then fluttered on to the next, to swing there and take breath between his carollings. You know his song in an English lane? 'A very little bit of bread and no cheese'. Well, in Brittany he does not mention cheese. He found that *fromage* would not fit his musical phrasing, but he will (so 'tis said) chatter to you of the *poulpiquets* on any summer morning.

We followed the green glooms of the winding trail, all tremulous with wild flowers, past clumps of foxglove bells, where fat bees crawled and buzzed contentedly, and then we reached the shadow-haunted pool. Here in the late gloaming the fauns and dryads keep their tryst, but earlier come the slow moving cattle to the watering, led by a goddess of untutored grace, white-coiffed, sedate with shining, dreamy eyes.

All this is true, for when you pass that way you'll find the pool's brink splashed to purple mire where cows have stood with gleaming sides and misty breath, the water dripping from their cool, moist nozzles ; and at the pool's end, where the path sweeps round under the thick nut branches, you'll come upon the print of small, hooved feet. The foolish might suppose this the spoor of Widow Ghouan's goats, but they abide, at least, a lieue away and would not stray so far; besides, these marks were never made by Breton goat, they show a hoof more arched and classic.

At this spot is a tinkling runnel screened by great bracken fronds and heather. Beyond, the ground breaks steeply away, and you emerge on open rock-strewn country. Here and there you will see a homestead with its orchard, but for the most part uncultivated land; all this the peasants call, 'the happy valley.'

We count words pleasant or unpleasing by past significance, by their bearing on our personal remembrance. I wish that I could change this name, for some of us cannot forget another 'happy valley' in far Picardy, where things that once were men lay huddled stark and black-faced under a brazen and a cloudless sky. But here we would blot out all infamy, hark back to living days of June, before the world went mad. Therefore we will call this Breton vale 'the golden valley.' And truly, for in the spring it is a symphony of gold and variant green. Then summer comes, and finds it clad in gold and black. (No, not the black of printer's ink, but that which the painter uses in thin transparent glaze to harmonise a gaudy colour or to restrain a glaring light.) In autumn this landscape turns to gold and rose, for at that time great piles of apples lie in the orchards, the hillside is aflame with sun-tanned whin and heather, brambles and red berries. With the coming of the evening light the stalks of dead asphodels gleam like coral, and oak leaves are as molten gold.

Within this valley are two streams separated by a long strip of rough pastureland; they join some few miles further down at the mill of Kastennec. We reached the first and smaller stream to find it alive with Mayfly. A big hatch of fly on such a brook is a sight which must be seen to be fully realised.

The larvæ for the past two years have spent a drab existence within the riverbed, but now, with the warmth of a second summer season, they work to the surface, and emerge in the *sub-imago*, or first winged state known as the *green drake.* But it is only the female who changes her clothes openly upon the river's brim, unlacing her caddis corsets, and arranging her 'transformation' for all the world to see. The male, on the other hand, is something of a poltroon; moreover, he hates to get his feet wet, so crawls up the nearest reed stem on to the bank, and then he hatches, after which he seldom ventures over the water, but hurries off inland as fast as he can flutter. There, with swift and unerring instinct, the lady seeks him out, willy-nilly he must become the father of her children. In point of fact, this is the serio-comedy of 'Man and Superman' as played in Mayfly land. So is Mr. Bernard Shaw vindicated even in the insect world.

After the brief honeymoon is passed, the lady returns to the riverside. (We hear no more of her luckless spouse.) She is now known as the *grey drake*, a buxom dame with all the airs and assurance of a wedded woman; further, she is about to become a mother. A few minutes more will see her hovering above the river, dropping her eggs in one by one. She has, indeed, a most prodigious family! Yet have they many enemies, and roving sticklebacks will thin their ranks during the two years that they must remain in the soft gravel nursery. The old drake is now growing weary, her birth-flights slow. Lower and lower she falls, till at length she sinks inanimate upon the water. It is then that, with wings outstretched, she floats away down-stream as the spent gnat. This final phase provides food for the fish; but it is while undergoing the earlier, *sub-imago* change that the female is most freely taken by the trout, while swallows and birds of all kinds devour the Mayfly in their hundreds.

Here on our little brook fat *green drake*s were fluttering everywhere, crawling up the reed stems, hovering above the alder bushes, and floating gaily down the sun-capped ripple where the fish were rising furiously. Alas! These trout are only small ones; this golden, shallow brook holds but fingerlings, eight to the pound. They would be fun with an 00 midge on finest drawn point; but now we were out for bigger game, and a great Marquis on stout gut amongst these small fry seemed coarse and out of place. We caught ten and returned nine, and then I moved on across the pastures and reached the larger stream. Here all was quiet, not a fish broke surface, and curiously enough, though such a short distance away, not a single Mayfly floated on this water. High overhead a swarm of undertakers soared and dipped continuously in their weird 'dance of death.' Apparently their carnival was over, and we arrived too late. Yet what a stream it was, with those long oily runs between the starry white-flowered weeds, and those green slow moving depths under the willow trees. Just the water to hold big fish. The only thing to be done was to sit down and wait patiently for those big fish to rise. The grass was soft and fragrant. Now and again a dabchick would move amongst the masses of white water ranunculus, or a skimming swallow dint the river's surface to form a widening circle, bearing a short-lived hope. Once a pearl-throated ouzel splashed in the shadows, but never once a trout.

The stream some distance higher up is fast flowing, with shallow goils and amber stickles. In turn were these all carefully fished with a spent gnat, and no result. Eventually I returned to sit again and watch in the shade of the same willow tree. The dabchicks still bobbed up and down amidst the weed to tantalise by poignant hint, breaking the monotony of silence. The day was very hot, the midges tiresome. Jean Pierre had got my landing net. He knew perfectly well that I should need it if I hooked one of these problematical trout of which I had heard so much. He evidently preferred to catch fingerlings. By now he must have murdered some dozens at least, and not a quarter-pounder among the lot. I was perspiring, tired, and very cross. I could not then appreciate the fact that there are worse places in which to while away the hours of such a day than the green shade of that deep-grassed riverbank; but Nature was sympathetic; despite the gnats and heat I fell asleep.

Some half-hour later, blinking through the sunlight, I marked the coming of Jean Pierre. Apparently he was heading a triumphal procession. My landing net was held on high, and behind him marched Mariic and Suzanne, carrying various cardboard boxes and an improvised butterfly net. Jean Pierre was hot, damp, and smiling. His pockets bulged, and as we watched, from out his person a few Mayflies escaped to hover in halo round his head. Then he explained. It had taken some time to go to the farm and procure boxes and an extra net, even longer to catch a sufficient quantity of bait. True, the big fish were not moving, there was no hatch of fly; why, then we must create a hatch of fly, after that our fish would rise and feed on them.

My old friend is wise in the ways of all creatures which move beneath the waters, and yet this theory of his seemed over-sanguine. I confess I was somewhat sceptical as I followed him up to the head of that long, deep reach to sit with Mariic and Suzanne while he commenced operations.

First Jean Pierre took a tin of Mayflies from his pocket, emptying them into the butterfly net, which was then twisted over and soused in the river. Jean Pierre and Nature do not commence their tactics on the surface, so this first batch of fly must travel down as submerged as possible. The net was now lowered till it rested on the gravel bed, its open mouth against the stream ; from time to time it turned for a moment to allow the current to carry off a few of the insects. Lying full-length on the bank and looking down through the clear water, one could see the flies quite plainly, but not their wings, which were so sodden and flattened as to be practically invisible. In fact, each full-fledged drake was made to play, very creditably, the role of hatching nymph. Batches of fly continued to enter the net and follow each other in increasing numbers, borne along in the slowly moving current. At length I imagined I saw a faint grey flash from the depths some distance below. Then came the suggestion of a swirl in the shadow of the willow trees. Jean Pierre had seen it, too, for the next lot of fly were allowed to float upon the surface. As the vanguard of that argosy bobbed into the shade of the first willow it was seized by a rising trout. I sprang for my rod, but Jean Pierre waved me back. Things must be done decently and in order. Three fish at least must be steadily feeding before we could think of commencing to fish for them.

Then a trout rose almost under our feet, just sipping the fly from the scarcely ruffled surface. At the edge of a weed bed a great fish came up with a boil and another fly vanished. A third trout was assiduously sucking away a few yards below, and. there were informative oily swirls some distance down the far bank.

It was then that Jean Pierre laid hold of the landing net, then that Suzanne was allowed to grasp the last and largest cardboard box. Her instructions were terse, ruthless, and complete. Only one half-inch must the lid be raised. As each fly crawled out must his head be firmly pinched, his not too agile person cast upon the waters. Equably, one by one, must these victims reach the voracious trout while we attacked some hundred yards below.

What need to recount the crowded hour which followed? All of us, sometime or other, must have known the joys of a Mayfly carnival. Moreover, the interest of that day lay not so much in the actual catching of the fish as in the way they were induced to feed, in spite of their sulky humour.

The account of Jean Pierre's miraculous hatch of fly may sound incredible, yet it can be vouched for by one who actually saw the feat performed; and I believe, given a sufficient quantity of Mayflies to allure the fish, that a similar artificial rise could be created on any of our southern chalk streams. If we carry the theory of these tactics a little further there will come a day when we shall have our hatch of Duns and Spinners to time and order, so shall we bring about our own damnation and ruin the delightful uncertainty of the game.

The bag that day was not excessive, yet we took four and a

half brace within that length of river, the best fish being just
under two pounds. Of course, we failed to land the really big
one, but then (as many fishers know), that always seems to
happen. His loss must ever remain a poignant memory. His
weight we dare not estimate aloud. At times Jean Pierre and I
still speak of him in whispers, my old friend's arms stretched
wide. He was a great fish, and put up a royal fight. Through
all its length and strife our good luck held uncannily, cutting
for us a pathway through the weeds, guiding the line through
countless snags of sunken root and bramble. Only when the
battle was really won, the great fish lying in all his glorious
spotted length, dead-beat upon the surface, only then did
fate play us false. That moment stands clear-cut. The whole
scene focussed in a small Mayfly, rosy with sunlight, securely
imbedded in a great open jaw. I see the lowering landing net,
Jean Pierre's strong arm stretched out; above, the arched rod
strung by the tense line, the taut gut, frayed by the snags
and perilously whitened at its finer end, the sun-touched
fly confident, secure. Then fate laughed. The cast snapped.
Slowly the great fish rolled over and sank like a phantom in
the depths.

With thoughts too full for speech we made our way
through lush grass and fields of ox-eyed daisies to the upper
water. Here fate relented, for on a wet fly, well sunk, we took
another brace. Both were good fish; yet what recked we – we
who had lost the king of fishes only one short hour ago? It
was then, too, that we became aware of the urgent pangs
of hunger, that lunch had been omitted, and that now the
hour was close on five o'clock. Fortunately, the farm was
near at hand (moreover, none may compare with Suzanne's
mother in the matter of cooking trout). It is known – this
farm – as *Ty ar Spaniol*. You reach it by a path crossing
a low stone bridge, up a rough avenue of walnut-trees. The
house of the Spaniard is three-storied, built of time-worn
brick, incongruous and un-Breton, but strangely fascinating.

A round tower intersects the straight facade, with loopholes at its summit, and just below the largest window spans the angle, capped by a pent roof of lichen-covered stone. Yet all the windows are unexpected, there are not two alike. For the most part they are shutterless, unscreened; but here and there are wooden shutters rain-washed, faded to the colour of hedge-sparrows' eggs, still hanging athwart the rich glow of the mellow brickwork. You reach the main portal in the tower by three great foot-worn steps of stone. You will find upon its lintel rudely cut its date, 1601. Can't you see our Spaniard the first evening of his residence carving in the soft sandstone those figures with bejewelled *puñal*? Suppose him swarthy, long, and lean. Give him a pointed beard, black as his eyes, a trick of glancing o'er his shoulder with a wild and hunted look, a dress of laced velvet, fine, but a trifle tarnished and travel-worn. You must know he built this house and sojourned in these parts, so rumour has it, *pour la chasse*. Yet surely the Spanish *sierras* held better game, and were not so far afield for purposes of sport. The peasants can tell us nothing, save that a *grand-seigneur* from Spain once built this house of bricks, and here he died. We know so little; even his name is lost. There is no clue in the ancient church records nor likely stone within the cemetery.

Only there is, behind the house, a small walled garden, a place of soft green peace and dappled sunlight, where old-fashioned flowers now bloom untended. There you will find an overgrowth of musk-scented rose, rosemary, and thyme, and below that small flower that the French call *désespoir-du-peintre* (in England we style it 'London-pride'). Perhaps the Spaniard named it just 'despair,' who knows? Amongst the tangle stands a nameless grave, bearing a following date, 1621. It may be that this Spaniard had a favourite hound, who knows? Alas! We know so little. Had he no kith or kin when he came (I had almost written *fled*, for Suzanne and I between us have worked his history out. It is very secret.

Suzanne, moreover, is certain it is true) to sad grey Brittany? Was there no other who once upon a time looked out above that window-bar, gazing with languorous woman eyes across this valley, through river mists of twilight, far away to gay Seville? This lady, did she wear a black mantilla, and at her bosom swooned a red, red rose? You see, with such a setting, the story must have a touch of sadness; we should not make it commonplace, or leave our Spaniard and his senora in smug connubial bliss the while they quaff a vino de garrote or share a succulent tortilla within the great farm kitchen. There at this very moment our fish are cooking, and Suzanne's mother is preparing a rich and tawny sauce. So while the trout are sizzling we will explore the house.

We mount the spiral staircase in the tower, its arched roof and rose-bricked walls so clean and clearcut, they might have been fashioned only yesterday by skilled workmen, to whom bricklaying was a fine art. Here are the bedrooms, large and airy. Across their ceilings mighty oak beams, joined and clamped and buttressed. The open fireplaces are lined with quaint-figured tiles. Doubtless the mantels are of stone, but all are boxed in matchwood, painted a violent brown (Suzanne's mother delights in paint, table covers of oilcloth, and much-beflowered wall-papers). There are great *armoires* here and there on bare and beeswaxed floors. Everything is spotless (with Suzanne's mother cleanliness and godliness walk hand in hand). But the walls are noisy as a patchwork quilt. Here first communion cards, blossoms in wax and tinsel, plaster saints and china *bénitiers*, all vie upon a paper crude and worried. Nor are these all, for every room has its *Ave Maria* in outrageous oleograph of golds and pinks and mineral greens, with every colour glazed. You will be sure that this St. Joseph must be the worst of all, till you have seen SS. Antoine and Etienne who grace the room beyond. Further, there are two little pictures in fascinating time-toned frames. The first might be a Ribera outlined in faded ink (you met him in Italy, you remember, as *Lo Spagnoletto*), and below an early woodcut of St. Anne. These two have found refuge in Suzanne's mother's bedroom behind the door. Indeed, the whole house tickles your fancy and conceit. What a place it might become were you the owner! True, Suzanne's mother has prerogative; and yet, did not that Spaniard come by a violent death and nobody the wiser?

What a place it might be made when, all that paint and paper scraped away, those massive stones about each open hearth disclosed, you placed your cherished goods and chattels (now warehoused in remote Kensington) just how they should be set in each right nook and corner.

But the top story is the best of all – one vast wood-panelled chamber – used now as lumber-room. Here in the autumn are the apples and green walnuts stored. Their pungent scent still lingers, blended with odour of leather, wood and herbs; for there is a motley array of old stamped leather boxes, with endless pots and pans in brass and *faïence*, mostly broken, a rosewood spinet in like condition and also out of tune, a lidless cedar box filled now with small wooden pins, some carved, some inlaid with ivory, and some worn thin and shiny with constant winding of the lace thread – not two alike. Here is a mass of 'trumpery,' a pile of faded finery galore (what fun must Suzanne have had here on wet afternoons!), bits of old brocade, and lace they wore on *pardon* days, a tiny pair of *sabot*s, a tarnished bandolier, a broken crucifix, a quaint cut powder flask in metal, and, best of all, grandfather's curious waistcoat of sombre cloth, with facings of black velvet. But just reverse it, as he did on Saints' days, you'll find a brave show of cocks and hens in cloth of gold with double row of merry buttons.

What a studio this top floor would make with its many cupboards and recesses and its long straight wall! There the old oak divan would 'go' perfectly, holding a world of ample cushions, and just above, well within reach, should be your shelf of books; and that great window – what a view! Oh! But there is a better looking north from the smaller window framed in crumbling sandstone, where the martins build below the eaves. From here you get the gently stirring tops of walnut trees, and then a great *menhir*, still as a sentry, guarding the *landes*; there is grey space beyond and clustered stone, and solitude as far as eye can see. This little window brings you back to Brittany. It was here that we learnt about it all, the story of the ancient stones, from Suzanne perched upon the windowsill, while from their nests above, the martins chirped in under-song.

It was ripe autumn time when first the Holy Virgin came to Brittany. She had often promised herself this holiday, having heard so much of *Bretagne-Armorique* from her beloved Mother, the good St. Anne.

You must know that in the courts of heaven everyone is very busy; what with liturgies, sacred music, and processions, one's time is fully occupied. Yet there are moments between the various prayers and canticles for whispered conversations. You can almost see those two, their heads bent close, Madame St. Anne describing every detail of her famous Church of St. Anne d'Auray, the while her soft-voiced daughter plies her with eager questions. The Holy Virgin so longed to see it all, that at last she took a day off and slipped quietly away.

Now, as we said, it was in autumn-time that the Holy Virgin came to Brittany, yet in that year, Nature forgot her seasons, for as the Virgin crossed the *landes* spring violets were born again to strew her path. Easter daffodils sprang up to see her pass, with wild, pale roses and all the summer flowers, and each had its tiny voice to greet her: *Alleluia! Alleluia !* From every tree the birds flew out singing *Ave Maria! Ave Maria*! to greet the Queen of Heaven as she passed by. From every Breton steeple rang the bells far out across the *landes*.

Said the bells of St. Malo:

'Je mets ma confiance,
Vierge, en votre secours.'

With deep-tongued voice the bells of Quimper answered:

'Reine de l'Arvor, te saluons;
Vierge immaculée, en toi nous croyons.'

Even the cattle, the fowls, and the ducks all paid homage; the savage farm dogs did not bark, but only wagged their tails. The peasants would have stopped making *crèpes* and pressing cider to don their *pardon* clothes had not the Virgin put them at their ease, explaining that this was her holiday, and not an official visit.

She loved it every bit, but most of all she loved the chubby Breton babies. You see, her Son had now grown up; His Mother's arms, maybe, were hungry, though the whole world knows how the Blessed Virgin delights in little children! Indeed, she had such times that day in 'huggleing' the babies, in playing *marelle* with the children, or in listening to the old folks' troubles sitting amongst them beside their courtyard wells. Such hours were spent, you see, on these affairs, that a waiting Bishop in the lane became quite agitated, fearing lest the Holy Virgin was running things too fine – not giving herself sufficient time to see her sainted Mother's famous church in every detail. However (to cut a long story short) she saw it all, and then returned radiant to the high courts of heaven.

So it came about that Brittany became the topic of the hour, for the Holy Virgin could talk of nothing else – the country, the whitewashed farmsteads, the costume of the Bretons, their ways of life, and, above all, their fat and dimpling babies. Everyone talked of Brittany. In fact, at the set time, when the angels and archangels, the prophets and the saints, took a turn together upon the sacred way, if conversation lagged it was always started briskly again by such remarks as, 'Talking of the Bretons...' or, 'When I was last in southern Brittany...' Then would follow a rhapsody on *la belle Bretagne* – SS. Fiacre, Guildas, Bieuzy, Sezny, Herbot, and Cado, and all the other Breton saints becoming very excited and all talking at once. You would have heard constant allusions to St. Anne. How well advised had she been to choose the Bretons for her people! How blessed, the patron saint of *la belle Bretagne*! True St. Thomas and a few of his friends looked sceptical, muttering in their beards about the natural beauties of Palestine. Another saint remarked:

> *'Je revois ma Normandie;'*
> while an old fat monk murmured something about:
> *'Montagnes des Pyrénées,*
> *Vous êtes mes amours!'*
> *but no one paid the slightest heed.*

Things came to a crisis, however, a few days later, when the Holy Virgin announced that she had made up her mind to follow her Mother's example and to build a church in Brittany. The building would commence that very day. She there and then invited all the good saints to come along and help.

You must know that the heavenly host is largely composed of Breton saints. Their departure, therefore, left the courts of heaven exceedingly dull and void. St. Peter was quite upset. He realised that, unless something was done at once, heaven would have no need of a doorkeeper, no one would want to come in! He foresaw an empty paradise forsaken for the *landes* of Brittany. Greatly agitated, he talked the matter over with St. Bernard, who quite understood his point of view, and promised to interview the Holy Virgin on her return that very evening.

Now the wise St. Bernard was a saint of long standing. He took a line humble, yet firm, rounding off each argument with cunning references to good Madame St. Anne. Of course, he could only recapitulate what the Holy Virgin knew already; namely, that once given this magnificent church of hers, once erect the Church of the *Vierge immaculée* Queen of Heaven in Brittany – well (St. Bernard shrugged with his delightful smile) – well, it must naturally follow that the shrine of St. Anne would be less well attended. After all, human nature was human nature all the world over. So it must come about that gradually her Mother's church would be neglected. Little by little the routes to Keranna, the ways of the pilgrims, would be overgrown with weeds, thorns would spring up around their sacred fountains; but, of course, the Holy Virgin realised all this. St. Bernard feared he was being tedious, he only hoped he had not been over-presumptuous in even reminding her.

The Virgin's lips were tremulous, her eyes a-glisten. Ah no, she had not understood. 'Is it not written,' she said, *'chaque breton doit aller au moins une fois dans sa vie à Ste. Anne? Je ne veux pas causer tel chagrin. Je ne veux pas ça.'*

Then softly the Queen of Heaven moved to the open window, softly she spoke unto the star-strewn frosty night: *'Je renonce à mon projet.'* The whisper passed along the *landes*, and every Breton heard. St. Fiacre, carrying a great stone upon his back, was straining across space. At the whispered order he loosed the thongs, the great stone fell to earth. You see it now, a silent sentinel above the branches of that walnut tree. Oh! But there are thousands more of these grey stones broadcast on Breton soil. 'Tis said they fell like thunder on the *landes* that night, and you can see them, some in long lines just as they fell, others grouped in circles, and there are those which were placed one o' top the other like great stone tables.

And so it is that good St. Anne still reigns supreme in Brittany. But there are times within the courts of heaven when the Holy Virgin looks sad and rather bored (we say it reverently), perhaps a trifle bored. At such times does the good St. Anne glance at her daughter with understanding eyes; together they pass behind the seraphim. They do not rouse St. Peter (who of late years has grown crotchety and somewhat querulous), but just slip out, leaving the door ajar.

Now, when you go to Brittany, and learn to love its twilights (there are no others comparable in all the world) – so when you go to Brittany and wander down the *chemin creux*, just as the first evening star appears above the stunted oak tops, perhaps you'll catch a glimpse of two figures on ahead – one is old, and leans contentedly upon her daughter's arm; the younger is tall and straight, of noble carriage. They'll seem to you just white-coiffed peasants, dimly seen in the late gloaming... My friend, our eyes grow dull in this uncertain light. But ask Suzanne and little Mariic what *they* saw.

CHAPTER V

NOTES FROM A DIARY

This chapter simply sets out to try and amplify certain notes taken from a fishing diary, in the hope that these may be of some small use to other fishermen in Brittany. Believe me, if the reader finds them dull, they are to the writer infinitely more interesting. Cold comfort this, yet how can things be otherwise? Can weak words convey a vestige of the inward picture of some special stream – an hour, a moment, we have loved? Can we give out a fraction of our personal reminiscence? Suppose that we could truly paint sky, water, and a leaping fish, the glint of sunlight on the riverbank, all these are impersonal. We have left out Jean Pierre's old beaver hat that always bobbed between the gorse-tops down every valley track. We may write the words of his one song; but its remembered lilt we cannot utter:

Ohé! la paludière,
Par ou done courez-vous?
Je vas à la clairière
Où l'on danse aux binious;
Mon bon-ami Jean Pierre
M'a donné rendez-vous
Pour manger des châtaignes
Avec du cidre doux!

Mon bon-ami Jean Pierre
M'a donné rendez-vous

Ma Doué! je suis bien fière
Qu'il fréquente chez-nous,
Le soir quand la grand-mère
Parle des loups-garous
En mangeant des châtaignes
Avec du cidre doux!

The words of the subsequent verses have now grown faint and dim, but the last stands out clear, Breton to the core... Surely Jean Pierre will keep his final tryst? They cannot drive the coffin nails too deep? No, surely we must come back again and sit amongst you round the fireside,

Pour manger des châtaignes
Avec du cidre doux.

The difficulty in painting a picture does not lie in the portrayal of fact, but within the interpretation of spirit. We may plaster a canvas with exact details yet fail to express a single truth. Painting, when all is said and done, is but an imperfect medium. The painter can hand on so very little of his own conception. I fancy that a writer must be faced with a like difficulty, for, as I turn the pages of my old diary I find, between the lines of ink, so much that is not mentioned and meet so many friends who are not even named. This diary contains for me much more than a record of weights of fish, of special flies, and certain conditions of the water. It holds a subtle intimacy.

I see again the small sad fields of Finistère detached by their high banks and pollard trees, their grazing kine drafted in miniature, spotted black and white, their little cowherds of blue short petticoat and snowy coiffe, who knit in the green shade of apple trees. I hear again the small sad songs they sing.

I see the dusty gold haze above the threshing-floor, the

wooden flails beating in unison, the priest's hands raised three times in blessing, the rich fat piles of yellow grain.

I hear the wailing skirl of *binious*, the rhythmic shuffle of countless *sabot*ed feet dancing the gavotte.

Another page is turned to a remembered patch of buckwheat that gleamed like rosin as the sun went down. Between the next leaves lurks the scent of clover buds, the undersong of bees, the fancied echo of a landrail raking the silence of the noonday heat, the winding fairy path across the stepping-stones, the washing place where the women kneel and gossip while they clout the dripping clothes, the village, the long white street, cut by its trailing vines and pale green shutters, and the dappled fig trees where old men play at bowls.

Here on a further page, there is this entry: *'Weather too hot for fishing; in the evening took three and a half brace – small red palmer as usual.'* That is all; and yet I call to mind that morning and blue-bloused haymakers mowing down the dewy grass. Swathe upon swathe it falls athwart the swishing scythes; laughing girls toss and shake out the hay ; their voices float across the river; and at the close of day (the taking of those seven fish is now only a vague and lesser memory) that unforgettable dank river smell when evening falls. The whirring churr of nightjar; the twilight whisper of the green leafy world; the white ghost moths fluttering in the grass as I came up the valley; and often at the coppice gate a lady met me. She wore wooden *sabot*s and an old brown skirt. (Lest this should start a scandal, I'll dedicate this book to her, should it be ever finished.) There were others, too. Mariic of the wondering eyes and sunburned, sturdy legs, and such a smile as only Vermeer has once hinted at in his chef d'oeuvre. Our first encounter was upon the bridge. Mariic could barely hold two plover's eggs in one small grimy palm. She dimpled at our bargain, promising more when we should meet again (as if such a bribe were needed!).

We swapped those plover's eggs for fat and speckled trout, and no one knew. There was sedate Suzanne, who came and shared my lunch one sunny day. As we together sat and munched upon the riverbank I learned all the dire doings of the *poulpiquets*, even to the one and only rune which you must use if you would sleep peacefully o' nights. 'From all ghoulies and ghosties and goggle-eyed beasties and things that go bump in the night, good Saints preserve us.' Ah no! There is another way, certain, if less devout. You place with care a bowl of millet adjacent to your bed, then, should the fairies venture in the dark, they'll tip the bowl and spill the seeds of millet; all will be well. For 'tis the nature of the *poulpiquets* to pick up all they spill. Thus, grain-by-grain, they will be occupied during the hours of darkness. With the first grey of dawn they'll scamper off. As they slip out you'll only hear the creaking of the door; should it be closed too quick, perhaps one squeak.

Then there was the widow Chouan. Her age was eighty-two. She called us bon ami, Jean Pierre and me. She told us wondrous tales as, after long fishing days, we sat before the peats and warmed ourselves the while she made hot fragrant coffee. Such tales they were – unvarnished, Breton, coarse and clean. I wish that I might tell them in her inimitable way: portray the whole background, the smouldering peats, the dark smoke-scented cabin, and most of all the play of light and shade across old Chouan's face in her narration of one 'Marthe Marker.' It was not a pretty story. At its grim end Jean Pierre spat softly: *'Bon Dieu,'* said he, *'c'est bien vrai – la vie.'* But, then, Jean Pierre is out of date. He would not like or understand our modern ways of life. Our quibbling plays of covered vice made comic would leave him cold or shocked. But give him the real thing uncoated, true, Jean Pierre would sit it through long after our Church and State had stalked out pink and scandalised.

Here have we reached the very confines of irrelevancy, to

place our friend Jean Pierre, incongruous, within a London theatre stall. Perforce we must leave him to find his own way out while we creep quickly back to solid ground – the diary.

On turning the leaves and comparing notes, I discover that the larger bags were taken during the month of March and the first half of April. Indeed, there is one entry as early as February 27th, when six brace of fish are recorded, the best of them weighing two pounds two ounces. Against this entry I find the following comment: 'Fish firm and in very fair condition.' This early fishing must needs prove a disappointment to the uncompromising adherent of the dry fly for nine days out of ten; though the trout occasionally break surface, they will not look at a floating fly, even a wet fly fished upstream leaves them for the most part uninterested. Yet if we are content to throw precepts to the boisterous winds and fish down and across the stream (and I would have you note there is some skill in this form of fishing, for Izaak Walton practised it), likely you shall meet some 'lusty trouts'; in any case, your day will not be a blank one. A useful fly at such a time is a fat palmer (old Izaak knew that too!) cast well downstream and worked across the current. The trout will follow round and seize the fly as it approaches the near bank. They will fasten strongly, sometimes with a boiling plunge, but usually well under water. Very few will be found to 'come short,' and once hooked they are yours, given a taut line and good management.

There are, of course, red-letter days, when flies hatch out and trout sip them daintily from off the surface; but these are very few and far between. During these early months the streams are bank high, the water not too clear, and the fish lying low and feeding on submerged insects. Apart from the wonder of the countryside, there is not much in this fishing which is out of the ordinary or much that the average angler does not know, and has not himself experienced on other waters.

We shall perhaps do better by pushing on to further pages,

selecting dates when the streams were clear and weedy, when the trout were less credulous and so more difficult to catch.

May 5th. – *An extraordinarily good day for this water, and lots of luck…*

A day of great grey skies, of open and unfettered country, where from time to time the shadows of the rain clouds drifted to leave behind warm airs and occasional glints of sunshine.

Not a fish showed or broke surface, but the sport, nevertheless, was good, thanks to a wet fly fished carefully upstream in all the out-of-the-way crannies and nooks. That is the whole art of fishing this water, to keep off the beaten runs of the poacher, and confine oneself to the less obvious places. Here we must avoid the perfect amber stickle, that on a Scotch burn would be worth a brace at least, and seek out the difficult corners beset with snags, the unfished water which lies beneath low jutting branches, the small hole under the bank surrounded by weeds and brambles. In short, we must fish the 'impossible places,' where even if the fly reaches the fish and he takes it, the chances are that he breaks away at the first rush. Yet fate is often incredibly kind in these apparently unequal encounters. How often a hooked fish, if not held too hard, will himself undo the tangle and work his own way out to open water. Luck? Of course. But then, experiment, subject to a certain amount of luck, is the chief charm in fishing, and it is a better thing to run risks and take unequal chances than to rise no fish at all. Indeed, the man who is over-cautious with his fly and unwilling to venture a losing hazard can never hope to become efficient or to learn enough about his craft. For all of us there must be moments when we reach the heights of tragedy. Such a one comes when we realise that the fish are only taking one particular pattern, when a dozen such flies have found refuge in the purlieus of twelve 'impossible places,' and we open our case to find the thirteenth sitting alone in cork-lined solitude. This is a time for iron nerves. No use to fish the open water. Our only hope lies in that 'impossible place,' and with this fly goes everything. Happy the man who can cast his last and thirteenth fly with the knowledge that within his pocket is a packet containing a thumb-vice, some fine silk thread, a few small hooks and feathers; for when the fish are on the feed, taking one special fly, the roughest and most homely imitation, if of right size and tone, will take them.

June 2nd. – *On our way back examined the bushed waters above St. Narec – no fish moving.*

The sole interest of this entry lies in the character of this special stream, and the flyfisherman would come upon many such places during his wanderings in Brittany: narrow waters, terribly bushed, very deep, with practically no current or surface motion of any kind. A casual glance at such a spot would suggest that it was quite unfishable. Yet these thorn-wrapped waters hold very big trout. Moreover there are small gaps, here and there, between the bushes, through which a well-oiled Black Gnat might be dexterously 'catapulted.'

These fish, as a rule, are not surface feeders, but on a rare occasion of a summer evening you can listen while one of these big fellows embarks on a cruise of inspection. En route he will suck in every floating fly and beetle that he meets.

Each cruising fish has his definite and fixed beat, so it is best to ascertain the course before commencing operations. Lying in the grass, you will hear a gentle 'plop' far under the dense tangle of overhanging brushwood. The next rise sounds a little nearer. Now is the moment to carefully take aim and flick in your Black Gnat. If the fly falls near old 'cruiser's' path, he will probably take it. If not, the fly must be left on the water till the fish has passed, when it can be worked into better position to await the second lap. As a last resort the fly may be gently twitched to attract attention.

June 6th. – *Fish were taking the fly for a couple of hours in the morning. Later they took a claret fly fished upstream, but would not look at a floater.*

The Breton trout has not yet acquired the habits of the confirmed 'bulger.' When he does feed, he dines upstairs like a gentleman; or perhaps he has been forced into good manners on the surface by previous unpleasant experiences in the basement, coarse underwater tricks of the wily poacher, sundry recollections of low-lying worms and beetles which contained an unsuspected sting. Yet might he not point a moral to some of our own modern exclusionists on their dry fly subscription waters? Each year their reports grow worse and worse; in fact, sub-aqueous feeding is becoming the rule rather than the exception, and the fish are being fostered in their growing disinclination to take the perfect fly upon the surface. The reason for this state of things is not hard to find. On these waters only the dryest fly is tolerated, and no fish may be taken under a certain size. It naturally follows that during a season, and especially in the time of the Mayfly, a multitude of undersized fish are netted and returned to the water. There were many more that were not landed, but these were taught wisdom upon the river's brim; they retain painful memories connected with flies that float. The chalkstream trout is no fool. He is, learning his lesson only too well. A further season will see many fish coming short, and more bulging at the ascending larvae, or grubbing in safe content among the caddis in the mud. Now, if for a season the dry fly was prohibited, and only the… but this, of course, is rank profanity.

Hitherto I have avoided all reference to the implements of the modern fisherman, but there is one possibly unknown to many anglers that will be found most useful under certain conditions. It is a bag of butter-muslin, made exactly the same size as the landing net. This can be fixed inside the net by a length of string, or, better still, by a few small 'dress-hooks' sewn round its top, which catch the upper meshes of the net, and so keep it in place. You have then an excellent contrivance for scooping against the current and ladling out any subimago, nymph or freshwater shrimp, thus ascertaining what underwater happenings are afoot. Nine times out of ten the scoop net will be found to contain the unsuspected. For example, on this particular day the trout had been taking floating Mayflies for an hour past, then for no apparent reason they suddenly ceased to rise. Yet certain underwater swirls or the faint flash of a turning fish indicated that the meal was still in progress down below. Of course, the obvious deduction was that the fish were feeding on the hatching nymph before it could reach the surface. My butter-muslin bag upset the theory; it divulged not the grey nymph of the Mayfly, but a small red creature. I have no idea what this being may have been, but in my fly box was a fly which, though not an exact likeness, was close enough to experiment with. This local pattern is, perhaps, worthy of description, as at times it is very killing, fished wet under bridges and in deep water. Hackle, a dark honey-dun; body, a light claret pigs wool ribbed with fine gold wire; small tag of cream-coloured floss silk tied on a No. 2 hook (dry fly scale). On this special occasion the fly was fished upstream, like a dry fly, except that it drifted down submerged in the stream and not upon the surface. This is a fascinating form of fishing, whatever the purist may say to the contrary; moreover, the exact moment wherein to strike is not as difficult and uncertain a problem as might be supposed, for there is always a suggestion of a flicker in the depths or an infinitesimal bulge on the surface of the water as the fish turns to take the fly. Here the strike has an added charm, for when it meets that live resistance, when the rod hoops and the reel sings, the fisher forgets the impalpable sign of a second before. His strike appears to him as a miracle of intuition, timed exactly at the psychological moment. There are days, too, when an oiled cast will be of assistance in detecting the trout's acceptance of the fly. The gut cast now acts as a float, which is pulled under water when the fish takes – only the thicker links of the cast are oiled, the finer point being allowed to descend with the fly. Here glycerine may prove useful. A well-glycerined fly will sink like a stone. Of course, as a rule, this method is superfluous, and we cannot be expected to carry the whole stock-in-trade of an apothecary in our pockets! Yet there are occasions when glycerine is worthwhile. A big fish is worth any amount of trouble. We must bear in mind, moreover, that it is the first cast that really counts. Number two has merits, and so in lessening degree has number three and four and five and six. But the first cast is momentous – worth all the others put together.

On that particular day the little claret-bodied fly, swimming a foot below the surface, was responsible for two additional brace of fish.

July 5th. – Two miles from the village car broke down. From the bridge watched an old peasant fishing with a 'grillon.' He got into a very good fish, which was eventually captured by the aid of my landing net.

The Bretons are expert in the art of fishing with live grasshoppers, which are placed previously in a grease-lined box to make them more perfect 'floaters.' These are not impaled, but whipped to the hook by a piece of fine thread, and fished upstream with a dexterous underhand cast. A friend of mine, an old Breton poacher, has assured me that a well-greased 'grillon' is the only sure bait with which to take the largest trout; once you locate his haunt, you wait for him at dawn. Before the mists have left the river you mount your fattest 'grillon' on thickest gut, and drop him gently beyond the alder-bush; crouching, you wait while 'grillon' kicks upon the hazy surface – each kick may be the last. Sooner or later, sure as fate, there comes the inevitable swirling snap. You meet the monster face to face... I only write from hearsay – not being an enthusiast in early rising – yet I have seen and weighed these trout over my morning coffee. Possibly the daybreak grasshopper might be found useful on some of our English waters. 'Grillon' might kill our great lean cannibals, those who shun all kinds of fly, and are impervious to even worms and minnows. True, this is no deed for the exalted purist, and yet a few words in season to a sagacious keeper might work prodigies before the mists had left the meadows.

July 10th – *Weeds tiresome...*

This I remember was a splendid day, the water in perfect condition, and the trout behaving in a most exemplary manner. In short, the fish were feeding in that normal way which we fishers always expect and so rarely witness. There was a good hatch of fly up, and as each sailed down the ripple it met a noiseless and unrelenting fate, the clean head and tail rise of a feeding trout. I had been fishing for an hour past, and had lost three flies and three good fish. Failure loomed irretrievable; a succession of catastrophes. In each case the same thing had happened. A rising fish had been marked down between two walls of weed in a long amber stickle. He had been stalked to within easy casting distance; he had taken the fly perfectly, but on feeling the draw home of the steel had rushed madly upstream, and eventually bolted for the weed bed. Once there he could so arrange matters that he, and not the rod, settled how much strain the line could bear. Gradually he burrowed deeper and deeper in the weeds, and soon there came that extra ounce of strain, and I wound up my reel disconsolate.

Then it was that Jean Pierre proposed a better way. We tried it. We stalked another fish a few yards higher up. As the fly sailed past him he rose and fastened and, like the previous three, he rushed oft upstream. Swiftly I passed the rod back to Jean Pierre. As the trout turned I had the line taut between my fingers *and before the fish had weeded me.* By this method we took a few good brace of fish while the rise lasted, coaxing, and, if necessary, skull-dragging each trout past those perilous, green, tangled walls. There was only one, a fat two-pounder, which almost escaped. This fish tried to bolt past us, and only by heavy strain and one of Jean Pierre's conjuring tricks with the net was he prevented.

My old friend has one golden rule for a weedy stream: 'Never let your fish get below you.' Better to risk breaking him with a heavy strain than let him past; once he has reached the weeds below the end is certain – he breaks you. Experience only can teach the value of hand-lining in shallow water and under certain difficulties; the extraordinary way a fighting fish may be led by hand to the net, whereas if he were played from the rod he would be quite unmanageable.

July 19th – *In the evening marked down a big fish feeding below the bridge... He broke me at once... was fishing much too fine.*

Now this trout was located, and then watched carefully while he fed. He was a heavy fish. I knew also that my 4x, though quite strong enough for the small trout I had hitherto been catching, was on this occasion over light. It might not hold him. There was, in fact, not the slightest excuse for fine gut, as I was then using a large Sedge. One minute's trouble would have put matters right. That minute was saved and the fish lost. There is among dry fly fishers a prevalent theory – to wit, that when we fish for an old, wily, and well educated trout, we can beguile him only with fine-drawn gut. Undoubtedly the idea is sound if the fly in use happens to be a small one. In the case of a large Sedge or Mayfly, however, the theory should be reversed. A fine drawn, dry cast floating on the surface is much more apparent to a shy fish than a wet cast of undrawn gut, which, by reason of its greater weight, lies in and not on the water. Moreover, a large full-hackled fly floats like a cork, and is capable of supporting a wet cast for a reasonable length of time without any fear of drag. Indeed, I have seen a big trout put down by a fine greased floating cast, and then taken half an hour later on the same Mayfly, which at the second opportunity was presented on coarse, but submerged, gut.

July 24th – *Woke to a howling gale; fishing useless. In the evening went down to flat water above mill; took some quite good fish... Alder.*

There are many such spots in Brittany, imprisoned waters above the mills, long deep reaches which under normal conditions are of little use to the flyfisher. Still, they hold good trout, and when ruffled by a strong breeze, are quite worthy of an hour's experiment. On this special evening an Alder was fished dry and *against* the wind, and each fish was taken by a deliberate drag. How hard we have all tried to avoid that fatal drag of chalkstream days! Yet here, and on this particular evening, fish were only taken when the fly was encouraged in its evil propensity. Earlier, and from the further bank, I had fished the whole length of water with the wind behind me. All drag had been avoided, and not one fish had stirred. Now the behaviour of these particular trout may be accounted for by the fact that they were lying low; they were not feeding, but were apparently prepared to come up and feed if anything sufficiently lively and attractive was brought to their notice. From the further bank my fly had floated perfectly but unobtrusively along the wavelets. From the near bank, thrown against the wind and dragged upon the surface, it was much more alive and flagrant, and, be it noted, the deliberate drag was not one of retention. The fly was pulled with the wind, not against it, playing the part of some buffeted creature trying to escape.

August 1st – *Weather close... water clear... fish very shy...*

In fact, one of those muggy grey days that we are so apt to designate 'perfect fishing weather,' as we perform that perilous early morning shave (one eye on the looking-glass while the other wanders hopefully towards the open window).

Only at the bankside do we realise the first touch of disillusion. There is an unaccustomed monotony of light pervading sky and water. Everything looks colourless, but very clear! The trout, too, seem possessed. The slightest movement on the bank sends them scurrying in all directions like waves from small torpedoes; from these other waves of fright are born. The fish carry consternation far and wide. Yet there are fly hatching out and beyond the bend we can still see fish feeding. With luck and sheltering bushes we may even stalk one; but the first false cast sends him scuttling off in apparent terror. What's to be done? We must think out new tactics, and at all costs must we keep as far back from the bank as possible. A friendly alder bush may make it possible to drift a fly down to a feeding fish in such a way that the fly comes first and the cast is not apparent. This method has many obvious drawbacks, but as a last resort it is quite worthwhile. Again, the cross-country cast may help, enabling us from the security of the meadow to pitch a fly across an expanse of buttercups and herbage down to the feeding fish under the near bank. Today we must bear in mind the importance of the first cast. The fish are too nervous to tolerate a second, so we must practise our cast along the bank, and get it exactly right in length before we present its tipped fly upon the water. Today mid-stream fish are best left alone, as they will shy at even the finest gut, but those resting under the far bank are possibilities and worthy of no end of trouble. Here it may be safer to creep up and then overcast, putting our fly on to the bank edge, and then gently dribbling it off at the moment when the fish is occupied in taking a natural fly. These gut shy days are never productive of much sport, but their difficulty makes for interest and experiment.

August 3rd – *Fished the water below mill at Kervily; weeds very bad. Tremendous thunderstorm in the afternoon. Took one fish, one pound nine ounces; lost two big ones.*

This was a wonderful day. Perhaps its peace and satisfaction are now enhanced by contrast with these noisy times. Surely even then I must have been grateful for that day's benison, for there were no motor lorries along my road, and overhead only one kestrel poised motionless against the blue. It was Monsieur Boniface who had suggested the expedition. At an early hour we discussed it over our morning coffee, and with the assistance of various spoons and forks and the pepper pot my route was demonstrated and explained. Monsieur Boniface travels in butter and optimism. He assured me that the river was not more than five short kilometres distant. He pointed again and again to the pepper pot, which represented an ash wood, through which I must pass, and at each reiteration the pepper pot slid perceptibly nearer us across the smooth oilcloth-covered table.

Only two short kilometres from the village was this ash copse, and once there I must be sure to leave the road and bear sharp to the right. Spoons and forks conducted me plainly through the wood paths; lumps of sugar, like *cromlechs*, marked my way across the *landes*, even to the proud mustard bottle that appraised the mill. Then from his breast pocket Monsieur Boniface took a vast cigar. This, I feel sure, would have given the size of the trout approximately had not fate, in the shape of a farmer, intervened. A heated controversy on the current price of butter then ensued, and at its height I softly slipped away.

The fourth kilometre stone was passed before the ash copse hove in sight. But what did distance matter at a time like this? I had the whole long day before me.

The green lights of the woodland were more glad and complete for the glare of the high road left behind. There was fragrance everywhere, warm succulent scents of growing things, damp verdant mosses, wild raspberry, sorrel, musk, and eglantine. The foliage overhead grew denser, set here and there with spruce trees, which gradually merged into stunted pinewoods. There were deep green glades where great lichen covered rocks lay clustered, where gold and copper-coloured butterflies hovered, pitching now and again to sun themselves on the sun kissed granite stones.

Here it seemed that there was deep silence, till the ear became attuned to the sylvan key; then out crept sounds and shadows of sounds innumerable, the faint rustle of life in the underwood, the distant tap-tap of a *pivert* pecking the bark of a tree, the hum of countless insects buzzing in the hot air. Friendly voices these, all calling to the wizard-uplands. Through a young oak thicket we pass to the open *landes* and all the joys of solitude. Indeed, I did not meet a single soul that livelong day till in the gloaming I encountered one old miller, and he was as deaf as a post. Yet at times as I fished there came, muffled and far away, the sound of chopping timber. There was a farmstead, too, beyond the wooded hillock; its chimneys lay concealed, but blue peat smoke capped the spruce tops and touched a homely chord. I did not need them, yet I knew that men still lived.

The river that morning looked perfect. Perhaps its waters were a trifle low and clear over the shallows, but they darkened to a tempting colour in the pools. The banks were gay with flowers, perfumed with warmth, a-hum with hoarse-voiced bumblebees. Here and there a swarded orchard stretched to the riverbank, interspersed with strips of heather, swampy in places between the knolls of bracken. There was a hatch of fly on the water, yet apparently not a fish was moving. The only thing to be done was to put a hopeful fly over the most likely corners and eddies on the chance of stirring a casual feeder. This can become a distressful occupation after a time if it meets with no response, not even one half-hearted rise. I walked and toiled and perspired under an August sun with no success, till at length the shade of an orchard was reached, and I sat down wearily in the long grass to eat my lunch. Ham sandwiches at such a time are apt to wear a dry and jaded look. The first did not taste appetising. In fact, it was never finished, for as I munched there came to me a sound, small yet unmistakable – the watery suck of a feeding fish. Again it happened, and again. Peering up and down the river I at last located him just opposite, close to the further bank, under a tuft of thistles and rising steadily. All that was needed was one dexterous underhand cast, avoiding the apple trees behind, and placing the fly just over and above my fish. This was accomplished. My fly imbedded itself securely in the largest thistle head. The fish went down, so did my second sandwich, and curiously enough it had a far superior flavour. The last mouthful saw the fish up again and feeding. Another fly was carefully attached and flew off to join its brother among those hardy thistles. Then followed the consumption of another sandwich. Things went on in this way till the fisher dropped out or was eliminated. It became a wild contest between ham sandwiches and Dark Olive Duns, but eventually the former won the day, for on two occasions a fly failed to grasp the thistle patch and sank upon the water. The trout became too eager at these opportunities; in both cases he rushed blindly at the fly and missed it. There were at the finish no less than six Dark Olive Duns neatly reposing side by side upon the further bank. The fisher regarded them coldly, vaguely wondering how far it was round by the nearest bridge. It was just at this moment when he realised that the one and only trout had ceased to feed. The friendly hum of insects had died away. There was an uneasy feeling all over the valley. A portentous silence.

I looked behind me. A great black storm cloud was moving up, full of awful menace. At the first rip of the thunder I was impressed by the fact that the shelter of the mill was a good half-mile higher up the valley. I started off, but could not reach it. The storm broke as I gained a mass of druid remains, roofed by a vast stone table. Here I found sanctuary. It was all extraordinarily exhilarating and unexpected. Around me the thunder roared and rattled. The lightning slashed across the hills. Heaven's waterspouts were loosed. The rain battered the river pools to froth, and tumbled in small cascades from between the giant granite stones, flooding my rocky chamber.

Gradually the roar of the storm fell away, and through it rose the sound of falling rain, and then the great drops were measured singly, less and less, to leave at last only their echo, the drip from the soaked alder boughs that overhung the river.

The sun broke out on a golden world, refreshed, touching all beautiful things to make them new. The valley was sparkling, green, and fragrant. Far away the grey hills still reverberated with the whisper of the storm.

In a near thicket a bird was singing in exaltation, and, most wonderful of all, at the foot of the mill pool three trout were rising steadily.

The fish lay in midstream, each separated by a few yards of weed and deep water. As my fly reached the lowest trout he came at it with apparent ecstasy; instinctively the line tightened, the rod arched and bent in those hazardous short rushes toward the weed beds, but at length the fish was turned, and eventually after a sharp tussle was brought to the net some twenty yards lower down the bank, a beautifully shaped fish of one-and-a-half pounds. The other two were feeding merrily, and my next cast met with a like joyous reception; but the fish was instantly fast in the weeds, and nothing could coax or force him out of them. He bore heavily on the line till finally he worked free. The fly returned, and was petted into shape once more. The third fish hesitated for a second, then ripped the line from the shrieking reel in an upward rush. Together we made for the higher water, and fought it out in the clear brown depths below the mill-hatch. This was a really heavy fish, and though by no means played out, he was well hooked and seemed as good as mine. I found myself excitedly speculating as to his size. Was he a three-and-a-half-pounder? Was he more? But at that moment the fish turned. Line was quickly recovered as he sheered for the near bank, and then too late, I became aware of another submerged weed clump. In those last seconds every ounce of reckless strain was put upon the fish, but like a heavy boat driven on a soft mud flat he cut through the weeds, and sank to rest within the hidden fastness. It was impossible to use a landing net in such thick growth, so I climbed into the river, feeling cautiously along the line till my hand touched the great broad side of the stationary fish. Another moment and I could have found a grip behind the open gill, but just then something happened. Perhaps I reached too far and slipped. Perhaps the trout gave one last leap for life. As the taut cast snapped his great dark tail rose once above the weed, breaking the surface.

The aftermath of such experience is too bitter to be spoken of. I see a lonely fisher sitting in tragic gloom upon a riverbank, gazing forever at a tangled clump of water weeds that sway and eddy with the stirring stream. Why, I had hooked the only three fish that dwelt in these waters! Two monsters had been lost; only the third, the small one, had been landed. This was not strictly true; there still remained that fish below those thistle heads. It was certain that he was still feeding. Crossing by way of the mill hatch I followed down the further bank.

There, sure enough, I found my trout hard at it. First, on all fours, and very tenderly, I retrieved my small hatch of Dark Olive Duns. All the while the enthusiast sucked and splashed a yard below my hand. Then, creeping back, the latest Dun was fastened to the cast and pitched upon the waters. My insistent friend had it at once, and after a short fight he was safely netted, a plump half-pounder. In Brittany we do not return a half-pound fish, nor yet a quarter-pounder. But this fellow had given me so much fun. Surely he should be the exception! Besides, he had kept guard and marked my Olive Duns for two long hours. The Druid stones loomed grey across the river. Perhaps it was superstition. Yet might not his grandsire be lured again at a more propitious season if I let him go. He slipped between my fingers and slithered off into the depths.

The shadows were lengthening down the golden valley, and so I started oft across country, making a beeline for a familiar spire that in the far distance cut the edge of the *landes*. On my return I found Monsieur Boniface taking his absinthe at a small green table outside the inn. He enveloped me with his optimistic smile.

'Ah, surely Monsieur has done great things on such a day!'

I had walked at least twenty kilometres, and was very tired. I was inclined, moreover, to be resentful at those pepper pot estimates of distance.

Monsieur Boniface was solicitous. 'But surely – surely Monsieur has taken something! Perhaps it was a trifle further than suggested, but to an ardent fisher a few steps more or less is a mere *"bagatelle"* Ah, Monsieur, do not keep me longer in suspense, and I have waited over an hour to accompany you to dinner! Hand me your bag!'

I lifted it off my shoulders and Monsieur Boniface seized it eagerly, fumbling in its depths till he produced my one trout.

'But this is magnificent!' he remarked sententiously, laying the fish upon the table. 'Henri, Marie, Madame!'

The whole staff of the inn emerged from the kitchen. Monsieur Boniface's manner was impressive.

'This,' he said, pointing, 'is a splendid fish; I had no idea our Breton waters contained such monsters. I estimate it at well over three pounds, and my friend is to be greatly congratulated on such a capture.' We bowed. 'Madame,' he continued, 'we shall eat this fish for dinner, and while you prepare it I will join Monsieur in just one more Pernod.'

Madame and Henri carried off the fish between them. Monsieur Boniface's voice waylaid them at the door.

'Madame, you will fry that fish in the freshest of butter; but before doing so you will please give him a *goût* of white wine. No, not a drink, just a *goût*, precisely enough, as it were, to anoint him internally and make him merry: after that, Madame, butter, the best of butter.'

CHAPTER VI

AN AUTUMN FISHING

'*IL faut cultiver son jardin*,' said the wise Voltaire, thereby bequeathing to distressed humanity the ultimate word in human experience.

Mankind today is coming to a like conclusion. Amidst the blatant reek of war, with all its weariness, its brute stupidity, its pain, its quivering wounds, its long scarred lines of trenches – amidst all these man glimpses his rightful heritage – a flower kingdom far, far more real and less unkind. These are poor pigmy times despite the giant guns and high explosives. We in France are not persuaded by smug platitude, nor have we found this war a cleansing fire – but rather an eruption of bestial materialism, which though it cannot crush out man's innate goodness, yet brings to the surface those traits which are most vile. Still one thing is certain: today we English love flowers and gardens better than we did four years ago. For us the markets of Picardy are gay and fragrant. There you may buy 'fried eggs and chips' at any hour, but must be up betimes if you'd secure the bluebells and the buttercups, the two sous bunches of clove-pinks or tight-wrapped mignonette – the Army needs them; likewise along the Army's ways are countless wilted plots, where pansies and forget-me-nots struggle for mere existence and 'spuds' do famously. There are climbing roses, tended with care, close to our front line; men wear sprigs of sweet william in their caps (in sheer contravention of King's Regulations, Paragraph 1692); even Staff Officers have been observed unblushingly to gather wild flowers. Moreover, it is said that once a Divisional General was discovered in a chateau garden, madly pruning roses, in the month of June. Rumour has it that thus were six Marshal Niels completely ruined – what matter! That General might have done more harm.

I have been led to talk of gardens by memories of Jean Pierre, and so it is that when we turn to other days, to Southern Brittany and its salmon fishing, one calls to mind a certain old world garden screened on three sides by grey stone walls, its fourth is rank-grown lawn that fronts a deep slow moving river. Along the bank you'll find a stone seat backed by a willow tree, and here Jean Pierre would sit for hours concocting lures or splicing broken rod tops.

Such a garden this – sequestered in drowsy peace and yet not too remote. For though the grey walls keep watch on its seclusion they leave in view the village rooftops, capped by the old church belfry.

Toward the broad paved walk you'll likely meet a strutting peacock trailing a gorgeous tail. Indeed, there are two of them, along with three peahens. Apparently, these do not fuss on matrimonial questions, considering only the poise of stateliness and majesty, together with colour harmonies in melting greens and blues. They are, moreover, direct descendants of those who once walked in pride resplendent at castle Rohan. Time and circumstance have not subdued their arrogance. You should see these birds today, preening their glossy necks, rustling their feathers pompously the while they move along the riverside treading the rank-grown lawn with delicate precision. To the tired fisherman trudging home at twilight their call sounds friendly. When the water is clear and low and fish are sulky, then the peacock's scrannel voice is not a harsh scream but rather a melodious siren, the certain harbinger of coming rain.

But now, in our garden it is hot noonday. Under the further wall are fat and yellow gourds which sun themselves along with straw-crowned beehives. Further are sturdy blue-leaved cabbages which hold the raindrops and the dew, and then come rows of beans and leeks and succulent fresh lettuce. Just by the garden door is a great clump of tall artichauts, their purple headdresses accentuated by the background of faded wood. Beyond you'll find neat patches of parsley and mint with thyme and tarragon; there the wall is spread with golden lichen between the tufts of herb robert and dwarf saxifrage. Each cranny has its diverse tiny fern. At the wall's coping is a massed fringe of valerian, the colour of crushed raspberries and cream, where all day long gaudy red admirals bask and flutter in company with humming hawk moths and blue-winged dragonflies.

If you take the little path between the cherry trees you'll come upon a clear cool spring. Its waters are always flowing, yet so smoothly as not to disturb its most minute reflections. You get a headless stone figure of St. Herbot in his niche, reversed in duplicate. Each single moss that twines the over-spreading arch is mirrored exactly in the depths below. You would not know that these depths moved but for the sparkle at the pool's brim, where the spring slips down to join the watercress. Further you'll meet the hum of bees in misty blue of lavender, and then the curd flushed and very hot in the potato patch.

Surely '*il faut cultiver son jardin*' would be here a fitting introduction. Best not drag in our friend Voltaire, but phrase the adage as if it were your own – just like this: 'Ha-ha, Monsieur! *Il faut cultiver son jardin.*' Monsieur will be delighted, scraping the loam off his *sabot*s on the delved spade; he'll shake you by both hands, and then search beneath his threadbare rusty soutane for his snuff box. At all costs you must take a pinch, no matter where it may find its way; for now the old man is talking garrulously as he toddles down the nut-walk by your side towards the open lawn, the stone seat, and Jean Pierre – you'll sit between these two and hear their talk merged with the murmur of the river. Every now and then will a great fish break surface with a heavy roll and tumble. Oh no, although they show themselves you cannot take these salmon here. Many have tried and failed – with fly and prawn and minnow – and yet there is another way, on still warm summer nights. A branch of gorse well tarred will make a famous flare... At this point the cure always winks, and then will Jean Pierre chuckle – of course such *trucs de vieille braconne* might be practised here, where Monsieur le curé safe tucked up and fast asleep in bed

This deep, long reach is useless for purposes of legitimate fishing – indeed, the nearest catch is some half-mile higher up the valley.

It must be candidly admitted that this fishing is not first class, or even comparable with that of our own northern rivers. In Brittany, though we often fish for salmon we rarely catch them – and yet we go on fishing! What is it that constitutes the glorious delight of this sport? It certainly has not the intimate affection or a fraction of the skill required in the successful use of the dry fly, nor have we even the satisfaction of a perfectly timed strike. For usually the salmon takes well underwater; the hooking part of the transaction he carries out for himself. As Jean Pierre says, 'Never jab at a fish till he jabs at you; when the line is taut you may drive the hook home, but if you strike a fish when he *boils* you're sure to miss him.'

Even the playing of a salmon, though a back-aching and stupendous business, does not require the lightning dexterity and skill that is needed for a two pound trout. The movements of the great fish are ponderous, and though he pulls like the devil, his turns are more or less expected and are sufficiently majestic to give one time to recover line and await further developments. True – these may culminate in that horrible and sudden aerial leap when the rod point is lowered rather from fright than good management, while we experience a sense of cold perspiration coupled with a sickening fear as to our fly's security along the salmon's jaw.

But it is not every fish who takes to jumping, shaking his head in mid-air, and sending cold shivers down the angler's spine. Often it is just a give-and-take affair of time and muscle, with interludes when the salmon hangs, a dead weight, in mid-stream, impervious to the strongest current and a side-strain that would tow a barge. If we are honest with ourselves we must admit that the allurement of the game lies rather in the primeval joy of tackling something really big, than in its art and finesse. There is, however, a physical delight in wielding a powerful rod and casting a long line into fast flowing water. The mystery of the salmon pool must always hold a certain fascination. But surely the element of chance, the astounding luck of salmon fishing, is its chief enticement! The knowledge that although you have toiled ineffectually all day, one further cast may bring that greatly desired but, always unexpected, pull, which more than compensates for aching joints and weary dejection – no words of controversy can belittle the exhilaration and excitement of that moment.

The visitor to Brittany will find this fishing disheartening work if he attempts it alone. His best chance of moderate success would be to obtain the services of some local fisherman who can show him the few *catches* or probable lies of the fish, and so save the toil of flogging many a likely looking but useless beat. Even an experienced fisherman is sure to make mistakes on a strange river, passing lightly over some of the best places and wasting valuable time on others which are probably tenantless. Moreover, the Breton peasant is an expert salmon fisher on his own lines.

His methods are very skilful, and though they would astound an orthodox Scotch gillie, they prove most effectual on Breton waters.

There is a peculiar cry known only to the Bretons which

denotes the hooking of a fish. This sound brings other peasants to the riverbank, where they take up positions beside sunken roots or other snags and there thrash the water with whin branches. Thus is the salmon warded off dangerous points and forced into safer and more open water. In Brittany we do not of custom 'play our fish for some twenty minutes before bringing him to the gaff" – indeed, I have seen a salmon hooked and landed in less than four.

The tackle of necessity was very strong, but the rod was handled with astonishing skill, lifted over or round the most impossible thorn bushes and tree boles with never a moment of slack line from start to finish. Someone had climbed out on a prone tree trunk above the river and there waited his chance. It came as the salmon passed swiftly below. The gaff shot out and down. There was a splash and a 'got him' from the man lying full length along the fallen tree, and soon a gleaming fresh run twelve-pounder was passed back to safety, where he lay resplendent under the lee of a furze bush. Prompt dexterity alone could have succeeded in such a pool. An extra minute must have seen the line caught in the snags and the fish lost.

The local patterns of salmon flies will doubtless come as somewhat of a shock to the visitor when first he arrives in Brittany. They are indeed gaunt, clumsy looking creatures in effect, destitute of what we understand as 'wing.' Only experience can teach that they are here more successful than our customary full-winged patterns. For some mysterious reason Jean Pierre and the Breton salmon do not approve of wings. My old friend has sanctioned our Jock Scott, Popham, and Black Doctor – or, rather, he likes their colour but not their form. These three flies he ties in sizes ranging from 12 to 16 (Limerick 'Rational' scale). The dressing is very sparse and the wings practically negligible, the few wing fibres which exist being made to lie along with the hackles and more or less flush with the shank of the hook. He ties the Popham in even smaller sizes for clear low water, with a shoulder hackle of Blue Jay tied flat along the hook. A very popular local fly is one dressed with body of black mohair ribbed with narrow silver tinsel, tail of orange mohair, hackle black, and head of scarlet mohair picked out in a ruff. This fly closely resembles the Toppy of Tweed fame, except that it is almost wingless, the thin strips of bronze turkey which exist being unobtrusive and tied horizontal to the body. This type of dressing has been thoroughly tested in lower Brittany, and has here more than proved its superiority to the ordinary pattern of salmon fly. It is a moot point whether colour and material really matter in salmon lures. The more important factors would seem to be size and attractiveness. The fly should not be too small to escape notice nor too large to arouse suspicion. Again, it must be capable of a glinting and self-sustained motion in the current suggestive of a creature trying to escape. Jean Pierre favours small flies in any but the most coloured waters; but he maintains that it is not so much the fly that counts, but the length of time it is fished under water. Sooner or later will come the moment when the salmon 'wakes up' and then it will take anything which happens to be bobbing above its nose. His chief injunction, however, is to fish deep, and this of necessity implies deliberation in casting and the slow play of the fly across and through the current. A well-sunk fly can move a 'roused' salmon from the bottom, whereas a surface fly, however alluringly it may be 'worked,' will in general leave the fish cold and uninterested.

I call to mind the first time, now many years ago, that Jean Pierre and I together fished for salmon. Earlier lessons had been given along the rough-grown lawn and from the bank at the foot of the curd's garden. It was here, too, that I first learned how to extricate a fly which had become fast among some sunken brushwood in the middle of the river. An old fisherman's dodge this, yet of such value in the snagged and untended waters of Brittany that an attempt at its description is surely worth while, if it can help but one brother angler and so save him even a tithe of the trout and salmon flies that the writer has thus retrieved in days gone by. When my fly first caught on the further side of the snag the position seemed hopeless, as each pull would drive the hook further into the obstruction. But Jean Pierre took my rod, and paying out some yards of slack, he cast the looped line above and beyond the imprisoned fly. The looped line sank, and was slowly borne down in the current till it reached a point opposite to and *beyond* the snag. Then Jean Pierre struck and the fly jerked free. The pull, be it noted, was now indirect, coming from a new direction – not from the near bank, but from the sunk line close to the far bank. So was the fly plucked out from the snag, whereas each tug, direct from the rod, must have embedded it further in, till the cast or barb finally gave way.

Below the brushwood pile was good open water. Just the place for practice and instruction. Here the big fish from time to time broke surface, inciting the novice to further efforts. Even after endless attempts to imitate that overhead or the underhanded cast which, in the hands of the master, sent the line with a great serpentine swoop to straighten far out across the river, but in those of the pupil resulted in a violent blow in the small of the back, or a tangled skein which would often fall noisily some yards away from the spot aimed at – even these afflictions were forgotten when the next salmon came up with resounding boil and flop. Yet never once were my strenuous exertions rewarded by so much as a half-hearted pull. Indeed, Jean Pierre maintains that all the salmon in this reach are 'sleeping fish'; that they do not 'wake up,' or assume that state of consciousness in which they are apt to be attracted by any lure, till they have reached the pools higher up the valley. Be that as it may, it is certain that these fish are quite insensible to every bait. Are they, then, in reality somnambulists, and their noisy plungings simply the tossings of a troubled sleep? An open eye proves nothing – for the salmon must sleep, or rest, wide-eyed – he has no lids to close.

So it was that a certain late autumn morning saw us on our way to the upper water, Jean Pierre with his old greenheart rod while I carried the gaff. The village was soon left behind, our lane winding past swampy fields and through even more muddy farmyards. Scents of baking bread and crushed cider apples followed us, and from each stone doorway the children ran out to greet Jean Pierre. Whole bevies of smiling, freckled, little girls, full-skirted and white-capped; small boys in precocious trousers and broad-brimmed beaver hats; and all chattering louder than the magpies. There were, in fact, scores of those birds along our way hunting for worms and walnuts and fat slugs, and talking as they scratched.

Now when you meet two magpies face-to-face you say, 'Une pie tant pis; deux pies tant mieux;' but when you meet a dozen, you cross yourself and bow nine times. We left the children at the manoir gates bobbing with deep obeisance.

This great stone pile has mellow walls and tall blue roofs of timeworn tile. It is dead and sightless, its windows shuttered, its halls are still. In its gardens moss grows everywhere, and by a broken fence you reach a dark pinewood. In the heart of the wood it was still high summer, but further, at its fringe, you came upon a hint of time and change. There was a thin silver network of gossamer upon the whin bushes, and a sharp tang in the frost-touched air. But the hillside's blue and gold was bathed in soft sunlight, and below us the brown pools were clearing after rain.

The water seemed in perfect condition, just tinged with a golden brown where at the foot of each run the pools deepened. The fish apparently were still 'sleepy,' for during the whole morning only a single salmon moved, and he came up with an angry boil merely to turn sulkily behind the fly.

Yet it was a delight to watch my old friend while he fished, to see that long, clean cast of his – the perfectly pitched fly that searched in every likely nook and corner, or hung exactly, beyond the heavier stream, working in tempting fashion. The day too was wonderful. A warm dimness lay over all the valley; an autumnal stillness, broken from time to time by the cry of a ploughman beyond the river, or the chink of the chains as the horses turned in the haze of the furrowed land. Fainter still at intervals came the distant sound of a shotgun; and near at hand the constant swish of Jean Pierre's rod as he worked down the glistening foam-flecked waters – the click of his ancient wooden reel. It was well past lunchtime when at last came the hoped-for pull. A final cast under the far alder bushes resulted in a growing and pursuing wave which broke to leave a brilliant and fresh-run nine-pounder madly splashing.

Never before or since have I seen my old friend flustered while he played a fish, but on this occasion he was distinctly nervous. He perspired profusely while the crinkles at the corners of his mouth twitched and deepened. An uncomfortable five minutes followed, in which the lightly hooked salmon plunged and rolled and lashed upon the surface, while Jean stood upon the bank and roundly cursed him in raucous Breton. Here actions did not tally with harsh words; never once did that fish get the butt, but only respectful attention, and when he chose to 'slither' down the pool, then Jean Pierre 'slithered' too. He made wild rushes and appalling leaps just as he felt disposed, and then would pause to shake his head, like a dog who shakes a rat. Twice in sheer hopelessness was the line slackened, but each time it pulled itself together to tentatively coax the floundering fish. At length it chanced that the salmon sheered towards the near bank, and hung motionless for a moment to think matters over. At a sign from Jean Pierre I slipped quietly into the water, and by luck rather than good management gaffed the fish behind the shoulder as he turned... The fly came away as we carried him up the bank.

We laid him caressingly among the bracken. Jean's hands still trembled as he mopped his forehead and took an ample pinch of snuff, while I had to light a congratulatory pipe before we could open our bag to get out the *vin rouge* and cold chicken.

Lunch over, Jean Pierre was soon at it again, and his third cast was rewarded by a splendid head-and-tail rise in mid-stream. This fish was well hooked, and consequently was allowed no undue liberties. Each furious rush was firmly dealt with and eventually checked. Once the salmon tried a somersault, but met only the looped line for his trouble. An attempt at boring in deep water was countered by a steady and relentless side strain. Soon the vibrations of the rod conveyed the message that the struggle was nearly at an end, till at length the fish rolled over on the surface and slowly but surely yielded inch by inch to the winding line and fate. My spring-balance allowed him 11½ lbs.: a fresh-run fish and as bright as the first. A beautiful pair they made on the bracken side by side, while Jean Pierre fixed the fly afresh and chortled.

We fished on down some of the best water in the river, but did nothing. Indeed, Jean Pierre worked over a certain pool of good repute a second time, even 'backing it up' and again recovering the water yard by yard, till at its deepest part a salmon came out with a bang and missed the fly. Now this fish had been worked over twice with no response. A third time had drawn him like a tiger on its prey; yet subsequent and careful fishings left him silent and apparently unconscious, till at length in despair we gave him up. We were nearing the bottom of the salmon water, and at the magic hour when salmon most do stir – to wit, the hour of sunset; moreover, we

---

* Mary Morgans are the Kelpies or river sirens of Brittany. They do not appear to abound, yet there are a few in the district of Morbihan.

had now reached the famous pool of Mary Morgan,* beloved
yet feared by every Breton poacher. The river at this point
is of stately dimensions. The head waters of the pool flow
through a long and rocky channel banked by high heather
bluff; its tail is bushed and difficult, but in between there
is an open space, deep and mysterious. Here Jean Pierre
changed to a larger fly and cast it out in the darkening water.

He fished the stream to the thicket edge, then plodded up
the bank and began all over again. Halfway down the line
tightened and held, buzzing in the heavy current. For some
seconds I thought the fly had fouled a sunken rock, till the
line slowly began to forge ahead and Jean Pierre's lips to
purse and tighten; The pace soon quickened and we could
not follow the fish downwards; but eventually he hove-to,
some thirty yards below us, hanging dull and heavy in the
stream, till the steady strain from the big greenheart rod
forced him to move out and up into more tranquil quarters.
Here the salmon played deep and sullenly, never coming
near the surface: only the taut line was visible, hissing and
rippling above dark depths. The salmon pulled up eventually
in the deepest hole, and there he lay and sulked. That fish
refused to budge; the stout greenheart was unavailing;
likewise the heavy stones which we heaved towards his
nose and perilously near the strained line only induced him
to shift a foot or two, when he would revert once more to the
old position. At last in desperation I cut a long hazel stick
from the bank, and tying a white pocket-handkerchief to its
tip waded into the river, prodding with the beflagged branch
as near as I dare to where the salmon lay. This suddenly
brought him to life again, and while I scrambled ashore
he rose noisily to the surface; once there, he commenced
a fight which was as strenuous as it was unexpected. The
fish had the advantage of twilight in his favour, while for
some minutes he pulled and plunged and leapt amongst the

boulders. I shall never forget Jean Pierre's sigh of relief when we got him safely up the bank. Here memory whispers that he was not a handsome fish… Perhaps he was a trifle red – yet might that not have been reflection, for still the afterglow of sunset lingered in the sky? In any case he scaled a full and heavy 19 lbs. Jean Pierre and I were well content as we trudged home. The weight of those three fish seemed good and solid. Such days in Brittany are rare and far between.

In the village the first lights were gleaming. At the inn door we left, below the sprig of mistletoe, our gaff and rod along with two old muzzle-loaders we discovered propped against the wall.

Within was sparkling warmth and hearty greetings – even the old curd was there to see our catch and hear our doings while he sipped his evening cup of tilleul. The firelight played upon the dresser's many coloured bottles, flickering among the black beams overhead, where hung the skins of lard and bunches of dried herbs. Above the chimney's shelf the blue smoke wreathed from numerous dwarfed clay pipes that puffed and drew contentedly, their owners pushing back their chairs to give us place in the convivial circle. There was indeed a large company of chasseurs round the fire that night. The village baker who shoots for pleasure, likewise his cousin the schoolmaster, and their friend the notary. Also there were the professional poachers – fascinating people, rough of speech, thriftless, their worn garments patched and sewn with yellow twine, miserably poor, eking a scanty existence with help of caps and rusty powder-horns. They, like their weapons, are old and out of date. They live with Nature under open skies; they still see visions and at times are 'fey,' so meet, despite their poverty, some joy upon the road.

We found many friends around the open hearth, not least among them being the tired dogs, who lay with sleepy heads on spattered, steaming paws, before the glow; too weary to be roused, they gave us salutation by kindly flaps of tails upon the hearthstone. Only Corantine, the ancient spaniel, came slowly over – grumbling at her rheumatism – to place a wet and friendly nose within my palm. She cast a conscious glance towards the heaped corner where a sleek hare, some brace of birds, and two fat woodcocks lay. Then she crept back to sigh and sleep amongst the wood ash, to dream of hunting, and while she dreamed she softly whimpered in pursuit.

We heard such talk that night, stories of moonlit expeditions, of trapping wild boars and how were foxes slain! I learned the weather wisdom of all wildfowl.

The advent of the widgeon to the lakes during the time of heavy frosts; the signs which always portend the first great flight of woodcocks to the *landes*; likewise the peculiar voice of snipe that marks the coming of the winter gale. Then the conversation turned to topics of the valley, nearer home, touching upon a certain dipper who for many seasons has built above the mill pool. You'll find her nest (unless the autumn floods have washed it quite away), a great round dome of moss, framed in the woodwork beneath the broken mill hatch. In spring it is a house well set in order, with four white, warm and glossy eggs inside. These birds, beloved by all good fishermen, are only shy and wary of the remainder of mankind The pearl breasted dipper is, in fact, our patron saint – a pale star that when we go a-fishing flits on ahead, from stone to stone, to guide us to the fat and speckled trout. Always she stays near us, and when we waste our time on likely looking pools, pillaged by otters overnight, the kindly ousel leaves the riverbed to perch upon the bank; then, with many dips and polished bows, she whispers for us her note of warning – 'useless, useless.

High on the *landes*, some distance from the river, there is a reed-rimmed lonely pond, wherein dwell eels both fat and succulent. Now it lies brimming, black and deep, but in the droughts of summer the water drops stagnant to the mud. Therefore the frogs enjoy it and talk loudly day and night, but the eels get up and leave the place for fresher and less noisy feeding grounds. You'll meet them – any dew-drenched moonlight night – walking upon their tails.

In the still reach below the mill dam live many water-spiders. You might suppose on casual acquaintance that they lead an idle waterside existence. But just lie down and watch from the long grass – that little lady there, beside the weed patch, has spent a long and tiring day seeking provisions for her ample household. Now watch her as she hauls upon her rope of web, a tiny submerged handrail leading direct downstairs. A few seconds while she gathers up her parcels, then a frisk and down she goes. You can mark her passage by a wee bead of air that glistens like a diamond. This she carries with her to deposit carefully in her nest as fresh air for the children. Alas! It is a little sparkling lamp which guides the sticklebacks to dinner... 'The *Bon Dieu* was not half asleep when He arranged it all' – this from old poacher Guerik with a knowing wink. Then: 'Monsieur has also doubtless heard how once, not so very long ago, during a time of need, Saint Herbot brought the small red mountain partridges up to our very doors – not one or two as nowadays, but scores and scores, and each one plumper than the last. Likewise in the year of cholera... My father remembered it well, how in the people's need and poverty the Holy Virgin called the salmon up the river. 'Tis said they lay so thick above the bridge of Karn that a full-grown man might walk their backs dry-shod, from bank to bank...'

The old man paused, sucking at his clay pipe. The great logs crackled on the fire; Corantine still slept with tremors in her dreams of hunting, and as the quarry doubled back she gave one sharp, short bark. Then the old poacher turned to me again, speaking in his slow and unaccustomed French *'Est-ce-que vous avez le même Bon Dieu en Angleterre que nous avons ici avec nous?'*

The curé's voice hailed me across the room, where I found Jean Pierre wrapping the larger fish within a dishcloth, while he explained that the temperature was over-warm. He added in excuse that tobacco smoke was not good for young and fresh-run fish! But we all knew that a wet cloth overnight can work wonders on an elderly ill-coloured salmon. Everyone drew round the table where the great slain hero lay: doubtless he blushed the more beneath his snowy shroud. With brimming glasses raised, we gave the Breton toast to the season's heaviest fish *'Ilia mad.'* ('Good health.')

Now you of Tay and Tweed, of Bann and Shannon, you who may turn the contemptuous lip, boasting of thirty-pounders, I'd have you know, ours was a Breton salmon... In any case, don't argue with Jean Pierre. Once roused, you'll find him rough and irrelevant. Only suggest that salmon had a ripe, full-coloured mien, Jean will retort that he does not like your face, or quote in Breton counterpart such sentiments as these:

Your salmon are so fat and red,
Your chicken are so thin and blue;
'Tis plain to see which God has fed,
And which was fed by you.

CHAPTER VII

FLIES AND FLY-DRESSING

There are two people who should not visit Brittany for purposes of sport – the dry fly purist, and his friend the owner of fat parklands with stocked waters. For them this fishing would be one long disillusionment and vexation. They would find whole lengths of ideal water fishless, and on arriving, weary, at the cottage by the bridge, would be taken by a proud peasant to admire his drying nets. They would trip over night-lines on the river bank; and, while gazing through their binoculars for that reiterated rise, would discover only a barefooted, blue-bloused gamin 'groping' in the shallows. Often would they be forced to 'fish the stream,' and on many a day only the wettest fly would prevent an empty creel.

If, therefore, our ways lie in poached waters, where fish are few and far between, it is not from lack of skill alone that we in Brittany do not maintain the strict tenets and traditions of the Test; yet there is charm in this fishing despite its blank days, and for these the witchery of the Breton *landes* can make amends.

Here is an open country teeming with brooks and pleasant rivers, which invite our expectant footsteps and offer an infinite variety. If one day we expect nothing, it is likely we shall not be disappointed; but there is always the tomorrow, with its fresh brook-side leading on by boiling pool and golden stickle through lush flowered meadows to further rivers yet unknown. And there is always the fair hope that some day we shall arrive at a place, as yet unexplored, to find good fish strongly feeding and our own pet fly dimpling the water.

Meanwhile, it will be wise to discount many stories told in Breton inns. There are good baskets to be made in this country if only we have the time and patience to find them for ourselves. As a rule, the miller's four-pound trout below the dam turns out to be a two-pound chub. We must remember, too, that the Breton peasant, though an expert fisherman on his own lines, is not a 'dry fly man.' His ideas on the use even of the wet fly are conservative, and he can be of little help to us in its selection.

The Breton trout has undoubtedly a preference for dark flies, sparsely dressed; and as a rule, he is confronted with far too light and bulky a pattern. From personal experience I have always found that a hackle suits him better than a winged fly, and that he fancies a warm tone rather than a cold one. It may be that the average Breton stream is warm in colour, or rather, it flows over gravel beds, rocks, and sand, which are all warm in tone. This colour tone would naturally react on any floating object above, so it must follow that the natural fly, being very receptive to colour refraction (that is, less dull and more reflectant in surface than the most lifelike imitation), would assimilate an undue proportion of the surrounding colour. Of course, all fishermen are faddists, and this theory is only put forward very tentatively to account for the fact that Breton trout show a partiality for an artificial fly that is rather warmer in colour than the natural fly, as we see it, on the water. It will be admitted, moreover, that if an artificial fly be placed, floating, side by side with a natural specimen, the two may present identically the same appearance to the angler, while from the reverse point Of view, and against the light, these same two flies might, by reason of their diverse textures and transparency, appear totally dissimilar.

Of course, we are all anxious to obtain a fly which is the

replica of the living fly. The exact imitation theory is the only sound one, but it should be an exact copy, as seen by the fish from below, not as seen by the fisherman from the bank above. In reality these can be totally opposed points of colour view. To prove this we need not make minute investigations with a microscope. A living Mayfly placed floating in a glass finger bowl will at once settle the matter. As it rests shimmering on the water, touched here and there by the most subtle opalescent tints, its bright body and wings act as a series of mirrors, and reflect the blues and pearly greys of the sky beyond the window. Now, if we take the glass bowl and raise it well above our head, looking up through the water against the light, we find the colours of the fly have all changed. He is warm and honey-coloured, rather than blue and opalescent as a moment ago. Not only Mayflies, but the Duns, the Spinners, and their various relations, have rich blood in their veins. Their bodies contain a more or less coloured liquid, which is sheathed from the fisherman's vision, but is very apparent to the fish. We can never hope to obtain artificial dressings that will rival those of nature in effulgence and transparency, but perhaps, by using a warmer hackle or rib, we may, more or less, adjust the balance.

When dressing dry flies, we must always keep in mind the fish's point of view rather than our own. The trout looks up from below, and sees objects floating above him in silhouette. At all costs therefore must this silhouette be retained, and the fly-dresser's chief endeavours should be to imitate form. If form is our first consideration, transparency must come next, and here the shop patterns often fail us, reproducing the transparent portions of an insect's body by material which, though it looks right in colour and tone when seen in downward bird's-eye view, is opaque and quite untrue when held against the sky. Indeed, there are certain insects with such delicate and translucent portions in their bodies that it is, perhaps, best to omit these sections by means of gaps, tying only the obvious and strongly defined parts, such as the head and shoulders, and leaving the more subtle parts to the trout's imagination. Thus is the silhouette preserved. After all, every object is recognised primarily by its form. We know the giraffe by his long neck, the pig by his gross and rounded outline. These could not be confounded were they painted black or whitewashed. The same rule holds good in the insect kingdom. The narrow-waisted wasp could never be mistaken for the full-paunched bumblebee, however unusual in size or colour. Cannot the same theory of form be applied also to our wet flies? We tie some 'fancy' pattern which proves to be a wonderful killer, so fondly we imagine that we have discovered a new 'fly'. Yet watch it working in the current! Its curved wings lie flat, like a dark back. Its glinting tinsel body is as a silver belly. The shoulder hackle now looks like pectoral fins, while the tag assumes the shape of a tiny tail. We have, in fact, a little fish below us, the fry of stickleback or minnow. Again, our wet March Browns! Do they bear the slightest resemblance to the living fly? Are they not, when submerged, very similar in appearance to freshwater shrimps? In fact, if we clip our March Brown's wings a little, and then pull out the impostor's tail, he may do even better.

That wonderful little fly, Tupps' Indispensable, is perhaps less of a *rara avis* than we have imagined. To the fisherman it suggests a delightful lure of glinting iridescence, but bears no resemblance to any known species of *ephemera*; yet we may reasonably suppose that under certain atmospheric conditions, and from a point of view beneath the surface of the stream, it would actually suggest the prismatic likeness of a particular species as the trout know it.

The recent controversy as to colour blindness in fish does not really matter, because we know that each colour has its own particular tone value. It is immaterial, therefore, whether the eye of a fish registers colour, or what we understand as colour, so long as it discriminates between the different tonalities of various tints.

Can this idea be amplified by means of an artificial Mayfly? Let us suppose we dress it with wings of the brightest emerald green, and body of cerulean blue, ribbed with lemon yellow. The result, of course, would appeal to the instincts of a sophisticated trout as little as to those of the exquisite purist. Both would remain calmly contemptuous, and yet we have taken trouble over our little fly. His form and proportions are correct and lifelike, but the trout (the purist has rushed off to contemplate a 'pale watery dun') takes not the slightest notice. We may put our fly over the feeding fish again and again, and so long as it floats free and does not 'drag' he will not so much as shy at it. One of two things only can be wrong from the fish's point of view – this fly is either false in colour or false in tone. Here we may speculate endlessly, but till we grasp the fish's point of view we shall not really know.*

---

* Since these lines were written, it has been my good fortune to discover a most interesting account of successful experiments carried out by Sir Herbert Maxwell (see p. 130, Salmon and Sea Trout, from the Angler's Library) on an English trout stream with a 'bright scarlet' Mayfly. After describing the satisfactory results obtained with this abnormally coloured fly, the author adds the following: 'There was some difficulty in getting the dressers to understand that it was important that the shade of these flies should not be uniform; that there should be dark patches at the head and shoulders, and dark markings on the wings. In short, that a red Mayfly when photographed should appear exactly like a grey one. The italics are mine, and point very definitely to a fish's sense of 'tone' and 'colour value,' which in the case of red and grey could be practically identical; nor need we, I suggest, from this, argue that trout are colour-blind. Science affirms that the human being is colour-blind to rather more than three-quarters of the full colour scale which light creates. May we not also reasonably allow the trout his due share?

In our selection of killing and useful flies, it is doubtful if the professional, shop-made pattern will ever quite meet our needs. These are naturally tied to take the eye of the public rather than that of the fish, and are, as a rule, too heavily dressed, too opaque, and altogether too neat and spruce in appearance. After all, the natural fly is often a very sorry object when it floats downstream to its last home. From birth its short life has been one continual round of alarms and excursions. More than likely it was subjected to a rough-and-tumble with a flycatcher on its passage from the 'feeder' across the meadow. It escaped by the skin of a wing, only to be hurled into a clump of dock leaves by a passing swallow.

Needless to say, fineness and neatness are important factors in the fly-dresser's art, but not at the expense of character, transparency, and correct tone. We shall find, too, that we can improve many a fly by the riverside by pulling him about and divesting him of much unnecessary clothing, when a small thumb-vice, a pair of scissors, and a few odds and ends of silk and. hackle, can work wonders with the most gaudy and overdressed 'standard pattern.' Indeed, if more of us realised how easy it is to make a fly that will catch fish, we should get much more fun out of our fishing.

There is something about the self-tied fly that tickles a man's vanity, and so puts him in the best of good humours; and always there is something fresh for him to discover and experiment with. He begins to find interest, not only in the habits of the fish, but in those of the insects on which they feed. A certain knowledge of river entomology is necessary to all those who would follow the higher branches of the angler's art, and the further we advance the more shall we find it necessary to discard certain shop patterns if we would express our own individual ideas in the rendering of the natural fly.

There are occasions on which waterside fly-tying becomes a necessity; times when the fish are only taking a particular fly. We have nothing resembling this fly in our case, so the one thing to be done is to sit down, there and then, and copy the natural insect as best we can. Again, there must often be idle hours during a long day's dry fly fishing, wherein no flies are hatching, and consequently no fish are moving. Then it is that experiment with silk and feathers can become a pleasing occupation in the green shade of bankside trees. Such methods make for honesty; the fisher is not likely to tie 'fancy' patterns when he has Nature to copy in the grass at his elbow or beneath the water at his feet. Moreover, he is just busy enough to enjoy himself, just quiet enough to hear all the wild world astir. (Birds and small animals take a tremendous interest in fly tying.) While the river talks of many things – beyond are changing shadows on the everlasting hills.

There is plenty of practical literature which will aid the amateur in his first attempts at fly-dressing, and from personal experience I can recommend *How to Tie Flies for Trout and Grayling*, by the late Mr. H. G. McClelland ('Athenian,' of the *Fishing Gazette*). This little book is eminently practical, and will be found to contain all the help that the fisherman needs. Maybe, for most of us, life is too short and busy to allow of our ever becoming experts in this craft, and we shall, perhaps, be wise in leaving some of the more difficult and intricate specimens to the professional; yet even these can often be improved by adjustment and elimination suggested from careful study of the living insect.

There are many flies which the amateur can tie fairly easily, and these will, with a little practice, prove themselves more effective, if not as neat and pretty as the professional patterns. The Alder is a case in point. The standard pattern is tied with upright wings, making a more or less noticeable angle with the body, whereas the living Alder folds its wings, like a bird, on taking the water, and floats on the surface with wings parallel to and sheathing its form. Memory here recalls a summer evening at Guémené, where below the bridge we discovered a big trout sucking in Alders greedily. My friend started putting the orthodox pattern over him, throwing a beautiful line, but all to no purpose. Each time that 'cocked' fly passed over the fish, he rolled up, had a look at it, and then sank back with a swish of his massive tail. This grew wearisome after a while, so my friend came and joined me on the bridge, where I was roughly manufacturing Alders, tied on short lengths of dried grass, but with wings fastened flat and not upright. I dropped one over the parapet, and it sailed off down the current, looking a clumsy and untidy beast, but the fish had it, and he bolted my next as well. This led to argument. Of course, that fish had just changed his tactics, and was now starting in on a wild career of artificials. Any shape would now suit him. A fly was hurriedly extracted from a japanned box, the barb of the hook nipped off, and an upright Alder followed my last over the parapet. My friend need not have bothered about that hook, for as the fly floated past the fish simply bulged at it, allowing the standard pattern to sail on down the current in bobbing integrity. For some minutes, fly for fly, we played this game, a cheap one as far as I was concerned, the score at the finish being six love.

It was then that I suggested that the trout should be once more 'fished over,' so we took the fly still on the cast and forcibly manipulated it, tying down the wings flat, and clipping away all loose hackle along the back. From the bridge I watched my friend as he crept beside the bushes and out on to a little spit of gravel, well below the fish. It was a long and difficult cast this, up and across stream, but it was accomplished perfectly. The paid line lengthened with each swish of the rod, and then shot out straight over the water, the fly falling beautifully a yard above the fish. He came at it with a rush. For an instant I saw the gleam of his great shoulders, and as he dived that stupendous tail. At once he made upstream, tearing twenty yards of line noisily off the

reel, and as he came the taut cast sang through the ripple. At
the bridge he leapt under my very nose, then bored for deep
water and a rusted iron grating. The line sawed and sagged
ominously, then suddenly relaxed, a limp thing coiling
aimlessly in the current. I recall my first silent sympathy,
and time has dulled our subsequent orations; today finds
me interested only in that great trout's individual tastes and
peculiarities. He had eaten six flies made of Harris tweed,
strips cut from an old rubber tobacco pouch, and various
feathers extracted from the wayside corpse of an ancient
hen. Was our trout an epicure? Did he after each morsel
cough and lay it surreptitiously on the side of his plate? Or
would a postmortem have revealed those six quaint flies
if fate had not cruelly intervened? These questionings are
futile.

The discussion of method with regard to the tying of flies
lies outside the province of this chapter, and can, moreover,
be safely left in the hands of competent authorities. I would,
however, strongly commend to the amateur the advantages
of experiment, suggesting that he not only make use of
accepted dressings, but test any new material which may
help him to carry out his own ideas. He will find that many
of the materials now in use lose all colour and sparkle when
once they cease to be dry, while others are rendered more
brilliant by immersion. This is an important point with regard
to the tying silk. It may be of less consequence for a floating
fly, which presumably is to be used dry, but for a fly or nymph
which is to be fished wet it is essential that its base colour
should be harmonious with the colour of the natural insect,
and that it should retain this colour relation under water.
Experiment will show the transparency of fur and feather
when wet, and the strong part played by the tying silk in
determining the colour and tone of the fly. Again, it will be
often found that two small hackles of different colours will
together give a more satisfactory colour impression than

a single one of large size, which, individually considered, approaches nearer to the tone desired. This mixed hackle method is capable of infinite extension.

From personal experience I would strongly recommend celluloid for making bodies. This can be obtained in very thin sheets, and when cut in tapering strips ribs beautifully. It will, moreover, take a dye well, but perhaps is most useful when tied clear, thus making a transparent skin, which covers and preserves any brightly coloured body materials which the dresser may wish to employ. Collodion will, in liquid form, answer a like purpose. This solution, when thoroughly dry, makes a waterproof and transparent body coating. There are many other substances not in general use which are worthy of the fly-dresser's consideration. Unvulcanised India rubber cut in very fine narrow strips makes a lifelike body; so, too, does that cream-coloured material used for tying up roses, and known to gardeners as 'bass' or 'matting.' The use of minute beads for eyes in some of our more bulky wet fly patterns greatly adds to their alluring qualities. Not only do the beads make for glint and iridescence, but they add to the weight of the 'fly,' and so assist it to work attractively well under water.

I have often wondered if some form of glass might not be introduced in the making of certain types of fly. Could not the finest of spun glass be successfully used as a 'dubbing' for various loch flies? At present these flies have bodies 'dubbed' with fur from the seal, hare's ear, and the like. Our spun glass could be stained to every tint, and, at any rate, would have the advantage in shimmer and translucence.

Again, waterproof varnishes of various colours might be found useful and attractive on some of the smooth-bodied flies, such as the Dun and the Spinner. Perhaps, however, this savours of 'painting the lily.' The idea carried a little further brings us to colour pigments, and we awake to find we have entered the realms of miniature painting.

It is a difficult matter to catalogue a definite list of flies for any given place, and Southern Brittany, with its many and various streams, is no exception. This list, however, may be safely headed by the Red Palmer, which here, as an 'all-round fly,' comes easily first, and can be fished successfully, wet or dry, the greater part of the season. It should be stocked in varying and quite small sizes (on down-eyed Pennell hooks, sizes 00 to 2), and will be found useful fished 'dry', on an evening rise during the spring months. There are days when the Blue Upright will do remarkably well, and it is a sound fly at times when there is no rise on, and the fish refuse anything in the form of a 'floater.' 1 have found this fly most successful when tied with a very small ginger hackle, supplementing and mixed in with the ordinary grey one, the body tied in the usual way, but finished off at the tail with a few turns of pale-coloured garden bass. This pattern seems to appeal to the fish, and is, moreover, a fair imitation of the natural insect.

The March Brown has a big reputation in Brittany, but unfortunately I have never been very successful with it as a dry fly, even when a good hatch was on the water. The fish seemed uncertain about each pattern I put before them, in fact, preferring 'any old fly' of reasonable colour to those that were fondly considered by their maker to represent March Browns. Personally I feel this fly could be greatly improved by experiment and careful imitation. In a new suit of clothes he might present a better appearance and prove a huge success.

To the two flies placed upon the list I would add certain others with more hesitation, because I remember not only the times when they have played me false, but the impossibility of successfully choosing flies for a brother angler, who will also have his special pets and peculiarities, and may by experiment in pastures new arrive at better results than those which fell to my lot.

In an old diary used in Brittany I had noted certain flies,

and I here set them down in the order that I found them:

Red Quill.
Dark Olive Quill.
Medium Olive Quill.
Blue Dun.
Tupps' Indispensable.
('Against this I find in pencil, 'Tie warmer sizes 00 and 0.')
Coch-y-bondhu.
Black Gnat.
Mayfly 'Athos.'
('Wings should be darker; try it with hackle only.')
Alder.
Red palmer caterpillar.
('Useful at end of season, tie with dark ginger hackles.')
The Black Hackle.
('A local fly as used in Morbihan. Tied sparse black hackle; on thin black body with Silver twist; sizes 1 and 2.')
Wickham's Fancy.
('For chub.')
Governor.
('For chub; tied with red or yellow tag.')

The reader here discovers that my actions have often belied my ideals, especially in the matter of chub flies. Well, perhaps the chub is not a puritan, and has a fancy for the unreal and meretricious. Be that as it may, one always, when cornered, has the unanswerable retort: 'Oh, but you don't see it as the fish does ; he really takes it for the natural so-and-so.'

On glancing back to 'Mayfly' in my list, I would add as supplement another pattern, the name of which I think is 'Hall's Marquis.' This fly, dressed hackle fashion, is quite the most killing I know.

As for the chub, we revere him in Brittany as a sporting fish and a heavy fighter. On English fly waters he seems always to be looked at askance, and has become the object of our gibes and ridicule. Even the kindly Mr. Punch has chipped him, under cover of brave sounding verse:

There is a fine stuffed chavender,
A chavender or chub,
That decks the rural pavender,
The pavender, or pub.

The further lines are now forgotten save those suggestive of well-earned sleep in fragrant linen:

From sheets as sweet as lavender,
As lavender, or lub.

You may not wish to bear triumphantly old chavin to your inn, nor to select him from a bill of fare; yet in the Midi is he greatly prized, where cunning chefs concoct the bouillabaisse. The Breton peasant loves him too; and such a gift, in season, can work wonders with a surly miller, who for a fat brace of chub will smile and lead you to some likely haunt of trout.

For us fishers in Brittany the chub has become a necessity on some of the larger streams, where for whole days together the trout, for no apparent reason, lie in their rooty lairs and bant. It is then the hour of the Breton chub, who, it would seem, is a better branch of the family than his English relatives, for he takes a 'floater' beautifully and puts up a longer fight.

There are days in the late season which can still afford us sport, days when the river is running cool after the midday heat, and shadows begin to lengthen from the willow trees across the pool. Beyond in the golden water lie big dark forms, which move up and break the surface from time to time as fluttering specks float down on the amber current. The Breton chub is greedily sucking in his evening meal of flies.

And now, for the sheer joy of fingering it in memory, I would add a description of my last pre-war toy.

It was a cabinet which held a vast and miscellaneous family. For years such a storehouse had never been considered, and my flies had found their various ways into most unlikely corners. Some were secreted in old envelopes, where they lay in undiscovered solitude. Others again lived in a green cardboard box, along with various rakish looking lures and salmon flies, all much the worse for wear. There was, too, a vast tin box, containing a medley of conglomerate silks, fly-tying tools, pike and sea tackle, triangles, swivels, wire, gimp, and much more, along with various pillboxes, each carefully labelled. In fact, if one opened the box marked 'Olive Quills,' one would have found it overflowing with Zulus and Black Ants, and always the one marked 'Tupps' and small Gnats' would have contained a single and gigantic Jock Scott.

Things reached a crisis, however, in the matter of a coat. It once was mine – a good old coat, if rather worn in places. I called it my 'fishing coat,' and my family called it by another name. It had seen life, this well-loved vagabond; indeed, there was a time when I had, with some trouble, yet at surprising small cost, retrieved it from the village jumble sale. Then arrived 'the day.' The fly were 'up,' and I was hunting for my fishing coat. The coat again had vanished, and in it I had left a dozen Mayflies sequestered in its ample pockets (I found them three days later in a salmon bag). This decided me. That very night I went to see a friend – an old man who mends cabinets – and together, cheek by jowl, we talked the matter out. At first he was sure he had nothing that would serve; but at length, by candlelight, we sought the open yard, and there under the winds of heaven, among the roosting fowls, we found my cabinet in embryo. Give him but a week to work this ancient 'piece,' to cut it down to right dimensions, and the perfect storehouse should be mine!

Tonight there's magic, for memory, like affection, can brush all space away; no need for steam or petrol here. Remembrance waves her wand, and lo! My cabinet. I see just the corner of my studio where it rests. There, too, on top, reflected in its polished surface, stands an ancient wooden praying bowl my wife once found in Brittany, full now, aglow with coloured seashells, the kind that children find along the shore, golden and rose, pale daffodil and pearl – all tiny, and each one smaller than the last. Above are shelves for background, long lines of well-loved books: Walton and Halford, Bickerdyke and Grey, with my reprint of Dame Juliana, her *Treatyse of Fysshynge wyth an Angle*. Ah! There's Montaigne, bound in a faded blue; and here is old Voltaire, in gold and black, nudging a paper Thaïs of saffron hue. My cabinet is still in candlelight, but now its polished sides shine comfortably. We turn the key. Its date is – but no matter. Two long low doors swing open with a scent of aromatic wood. A triple nest of drawers, each with its small and quaint cut ivory handles. The first is just a narrow tray, cork lined, cream papered, housing the very young. The family of Gnats, the Smuts, the Tupps', the lesser Quills, a Silver Sedge, and here the Jenny Spinners. The lower drawer is deeper, wherein are Duns laid out, along with Hares' Ears, Coachmen, Alders, Blue Uprights, and Grannoms. An 'Artful Dodger' this, dressed by a Devonshire keeper; these Heckum Peckums here were tied at a manse in Skye; and that bright fellow came all the way from the Maine woods – you'll find him labelled, 'F. G.'s special, Rainbow Trout'; and, further, a whole row of March Browns, both gentlemen and ladies. My flats, you see, are self-contained, replete with every up-to-date contrivance ; each floor has its small corner cubicle, piled high with camphor and crushed 'feverfew,' lest fluttering thieves break through and steal.

The last and deepest drawer reveals a sparkling galaxy. All the loch flies: Orange and Silver, Green and Teal, Bronze Mallard, Grouse and Claret, the Invictas, the Butchers, and fat Palmers. The Nymphs with Mayflies in companies, both winged and hackled. Sundry attempts in the freshwater shrimp, and here an old frayed fly of halcyon day, that lured the father of all Breton trout, that held through weeds below the boiling weir, to conquer in the mead where kingcups grow.

Oh, damn! Let's close the little doors and turn the key, and with its click we pass from what is sane and real, as thought moves on to actuality, paling the candles' gleam, dimming the books along the wall, veiling the firelight cast across the floor, where little pattering feet were wont to tread, leaving the deep seats empty to the silence there.

The wind is rising, with sudden gusts that beat against the pane. It moans and rattles at the fastenings. It pauses, gathering force, then flings the French windows wide, bringing with it the sleet and the rain and the sounds in the night. For in the roar of the wind there is a muffled and constant chord, jarring, alien, yet ever moving through it. Again the wind pauses, holding its breath, giving place to that vibrant reiterated growl, falling at times from sound to mere sensation, rising again louder and even louder in long-drawn resonance – boom – boom – boom. The guns at night. I sigh as I think of the storehouse sleeping far away in silence, the wooden bowl atop, with tiny shimmering shells that children love.

CHAPTER VIII

L'ENVOI

The November of 1913 set in cold and grey, bringing with it the black, dark days of the *Misdhu*, and my last night in Brittany. For the past week I had lingered on alone at the Lion d'Or to finish a picture and to make a few last studies. Well, they were done, and tonight Jean Pierre would drive me to the midnight train for Paris. I should join my family there on the morrow.

The bags were packed, and the last strap buckled round my rods and painting traps, when Anastasie's voice rang up the stairs.

Would I descend? Monsieur le Maire had come and sent his salutations. Below I found him, wearing his bowler hat, agog with animation; and with him were the Greffier and other good folk who had come to bid me *bon voyage* over a parting mug of cider. We drew our chairs around the kitchen fire. I had dined earlier – a somewhat cheerless affair, alone in the long chilly *salle à manger* – and welcomed the prospect of an hour's gossip in the warmth before my cart arrived.

We talked while Anastasie filled the cider bowls, and then brought out her knitting, the firelight glinting on those ever moving needles.

Then in came old Morvan, the shepherd; and behind him another of my models, Ian Abalen, a wild-eyed man, a beggar. In England he would be the village idiot, but here an 'Innocent,' 'the guest of God.'

More jugs were brought; old Morvan's shaggy coat was

laid aside, while Ian Abalen, carrying his mug, crept to the hearth.

Again the voices rose and fell; the knitting needles clicked. We talked of bécasse shooting, of the last year's crops, the pardon of St. Anne, the curé's tithes, and suchlike village topics, and all the while Ian Abalen crouched silent in the inglenook, gazing beyond the glowing fire, his piteous mouth agape. If one could only paint him just like that! His rigid pose, his tense white face, those staring vacant eyes. Velasquez could have done it. But what were they talking about now? War that was certain, imminent. They harped on it, leaving me cold and sceptical. In these days – war with Germany – preposterous! These peasants should talk of things they understood – their sheep, their crops. In turn I tried every subject, but each led back to war.

Solemnly the Greffier raised his bowl: *À bas les Alboches! À mort les Prussians! Vive la France!* The toast was drunk. The china mugs then clattered down in unison, while grey heads nodded knowingly. There would be war – they knew it. 'And when war comes' (this from old Morvan, garrulous and flushed) – 'and when it comes' – he pointed a jabbing finger – 'monsieur will leave his paints and fight for France.' That nettled me, drawing the retort: 'My friend, I may be all kinds of a fool in this world, but not a soldier.' Old Morvan answered: 'You will fight for France.'

The fire glowed; a log sagged white in ashes. Then in the silence Ian spoke. 'I see,' he said, 'a whole world at war, all nations armed. I suffer the weariness of their marching. I hear the tramp of countless feet; massed ranks advancing to pain, and fear, and strife. From all sides war rolls in. Now it surrounds me, wave upon wave. It laps my feet, my side, my hands. Mother of God, hold back this baneful flood!' Shivering he paused, then with strained voice, his palsied arms outstretched: 'What shall it profit them? For those who gain shall lose, the vanquished shall be conquerors, and...'

The twitching hands sank aimlessly, the quavering voice trailed off in whispered gibberings.

Embarrassed silence held us all. Anastasie hastily refilled the cider mugs and heaped furze faggots on the hearth; the fire crackled, then burst ablaze, waking our talk once more, while sparks flew up the open chimney. The mayor bent down apologetically. *'Le pauvre malheureuox,'* he said, *'vous savez—le pauvre homme.'* He shrugged and glanced towards the inglenook. The fire cracked and roared, whilst weird shadows flickered on the wall.

Anon Jean Pierre arrived, my baggage was brought down, while the whole party trooped out to the inn door.

The night had cleared. A wonder of a moon rode high in heaven and bathed the square in silver light. With much handshaking I settled myself and belongings in the cart alongside Jean Pierre, and my good friends all shouted good wishes as we made our start. Anastasie beamed. *'Bon voyage alors, monsieur. Bien le bonjour à madame.'* The Mayor waved a hand. *'Bonne chance à la prochaine. Bonne santé, et Au revoir.'* In turn I raised my hand in a salute, and then looked back. The door had closed. I saw only one silent figure below the lintel, its long hair hanging straight, framing an ashen face, its wild eyes with steadfast gaze catching the glint of the moonlight.

For some time we drove in silence, each occupied with his own thoughts and the glamour of the night, while the white ribbon of the road ever unwound before us. Then at the breast of a hill we caught the first faint murmur of the river far below; further, we reached the bridge, which rang hollow beneath our horses' hoofs. The river here flowed deep and dark, gurgling and talking as it passed the piers; above it lay a long still reach of silver, backed by gaunt poplar trees. Beyond, the mill, its white walls shining, bathed in mellow light, its vast wheel motionless and silent. On again, up through the still beech woods to open country, half moor, half pastureland; and there before us, set in a barren space, an ancient Breton chapel. I knew it well, this chapel of St. Herbot. Many a sunny day had I painted here; but now in this strange light it all seemed changed. The old stone facade and the crumbling arch were lost, veiled in deep shadow. The fretted spire loomed big against the sky.

Jean pulled up, unpocketing a vast timepiece; then, turning with an air half grave, half humorous: 'If Monsieur would see his studio by moonlight, we still have more than time.' So out we tumbled, Jean Pierre hitching up the reins and following me up the stone-flagged pathway.

The door swung inwards. In the darkness above us something stirred, some frightened owl or nighthawk; its flapping wings swept past us in the gloom. The air was misty and damp-laden. Jean's *sabot*s clattered across the uneven floor, waking the echoes in the raftered roof. The place was shrouded in deep velvet shadows, save where, beyond the rood screen, the light glowed through the stained glass of the east window, filling the air with soft and coloured radiance. Instinctively on entering I moved to bare my head, when Jean Pierre's voice arrested me: *'Ça fait rien, monsieur; ça fait rien. Le Bon Dieu n'est pas ici cette nuit. Il est au Kloar.'* Through painted window the moonlight flowed over the altar – bare ; over niches in the wall – empty. Then I understood. Tomorrow was the saint's day; tonight St. Herbot, with other carved and gilded saints, slept in the parish church two leagues away waiting the morrow's festival.

Only the human elements remained. A model of a ship riding a dusky moonlit sea, a votive offering from the fishers of Pouldu, loomed in the choir; some waxen hands and feet, the yearning gifts of halt and lame, lay clustered in the shadow, and from a pillar hung a little crutch of wood. Jean Pierre tiptoed across the uneven floor; softly we closed the door.

Outside the clear moonlight bathed the world in stillness,

broken only by the creaking of the cart as the old horse steadily browsed along the track. Jean took a pinch of snuff, then gathered up the reins. I lit my pipe and clambered in beside him. Our road now lay for a good distance along a strip of moorland. On one hand the intersecting hills stretched vague and dim: on the other dark pine woods unfolded, and from their shadows here and there a few grey rocks crept out as if to catch the moonbeams. Ever a gentle breeze went with us, shivering the sleepy grass and dead bracken, stirring the treetops dark against the moon, bringing with it the sounds and scents of the night. Now the road dipped to rejoin the glistening beech woods, and further ran in between rich pasturelands, till at length we reached the chateau of Kermour, where on one side stood two great wrought iron gates, flung wide a-hinge on massive timeworn columns of stone, and beyond, a straight, long avenue of trees cut sharp against the sky, leading in vista to the ancient manoir. It lay remote, veiled now in mystery, save for a single window, where lights still burned. Jean Pierre chuckled. 'Monsieur le Marquis is a proud and happy man this night,' he said; 'only today his son returned from service in Algiers. Madoué! How he loves that boy! He needs him too; he grows old, you see. These are sad times for the *vraie noblesse.*' He paused, his whip nicked at the moonlit sky. 'I hate the Government!' he muttered. 'God! how I hate them!' 'And you a patriotic Frenchman,' I retorted, smiling. Jean Pierre turned swiftly: 'Never say that, monsieur, *jamais. Français! Sapristi non. Je ne suis pas Français moi; je suis Breton.*'

Now we were passing the first low houses of the village, wrapped in sleep, waking the echoes along the cobbled street, and then we reached the station's ugliness. A sleepy porter handed down my bags; we found the stuffy *salle d'attente*, with its ill-smelling, flickering lamp. At last the great train rolled in and halted panting. I climbed aboard. The sleepy porter walked the platform's length, intoning the station's name, like some *muezzin* crying from a mosque a prayer to Allah in the silent night. The great train jibbed and groaned upon the metals, then glided smoothly out between tall signal lights of red and green.

Leaning from the open window I marked the loose-limbed, blue-bloused figure of Jean Pierre as he stood alone on the platform, his old beribboned beaver hat shading his face.

He raised a hand.

That was four years ago. Tonight my thoughts lead me back along that moonlit road, leaving the station's ugliness and the sleeping houses in the village street to stand bareheaded at the entrance of that long avenue. Tonight no light shines in the chateau, and yet I see an old man sitting lonely in a darkened room, the last of all his line; a great name passes with him. I have his letter by me as I write, 'I am,' so run the trembling characters, 'I am today the saddest and the proudest man in France.' So speaks the *vraie noblesse*. And Jean Pierre, what of him? He fell in front of Verdun, rushed up with other veterans to stem a night attack. He fell in front of Verdun, a German bullet through his head. God! Like Jean Pierre, I hate these Governments.

Tonight the world is suffering, paying a bitter price in pain and fear and strife. 'What shall it profit them?' I hear again mad Abalen's voice. Tonight he counts his dead in a land desolate. For Ian Abalen, the *Innocent*, is wise. He knows that spirits of the dead return again to Brittany, along the *landes*, among the woods and by the waters which they loved so well.

Oh, Brittany, you are not forgotten! And I remember a moonlit night four years ago, a lonely chapel, a ship suspended in a silver sea, a little crutch that hung against the wall, the sound of *sabot*s clicking tiptoe across the floor, the door soft closed.

I like to think that when Jean Pierre fell St. Herbot bent

low over that whimsical still face that gazed across the shell-shattered waste towards the west and Brittany. I like to think that the good saint spoke these words of comfort to the parting soul, not with a heavenly cadence, but in a rough peasant accent like Jean's own – *Ça fait rien; ça fait rien. Le Bon Dieu n'est pas ici cette nuit. Il est au Kloar.*

OTHER IMPORTANT FLY-FISHING BOOKS
AVAILABLE FROM
THE FLYFISHER'S CLASSIC LIBRARY

-/-

A Salmon Fisher's Odyssey – John Ashley-Cooper
The Flyfisher's Guide – G. C. Bainbridge
The Art of Fly Making – William Blacker
An Angler's Paradise – F. D. Barker
Sunshine and the Dry Fly – J.W. Dunne
Brook & River Trouting – Edmonds & Lee
Fly-Tyer's Masterclass –Oliver Edwards
The Book of the Salmon – Ephemera
Going Fishing – Negley Farson
A Book on Angling – Francis Francis
Fly Fishing – Sir Edward Grey
The Essential Kelson – Terry Griffiths
An Angler's Autobiography – F. M. Halford
The House the Hardy Brothers Built – J. L. Hardy
A Summer on the Test – J. W. Hills
My Sporting Life – J. W. Hills
River Keeper – J. W. Hills
Autumns on the Spey – A. E. Knox
Salmon and Sea Trout – Sir Herbert Maxwell
Fly-Fishing: Some New Arts and Mysteries – J. C. Mottram
Fishing in Eden – William Nelson
Grayling Fishing – W. Carter Platts
The Book of the Grayling – T. E. Pritt
Yorkshire Trout Flies – T. E. Pritt
Rod and Line – Arthur Ransome
Flies for Snowdonia – Plu Eryri – William Roberts
The Frank Sawyer Omnibus – Frank Sawyer
Days and Nights of Salmon Fishing on the Tweed – W. Scrope
Nymph Fishing for Chalk Stream Trout – G. E. M. Skues
Silk, Fur and Feather: The Fly Dresser's Handbook – G. E. M. Skues
Side-lines, Side-lights and Reflections – G. E. M. Skues
The Way of a Trout with a Fly – G. E. M. Skues
Flyfishing the Welsh Borderlands – Roger Smith
The Practical Angler – W. C. Stewart
Jones's Guide to Norway – F. Tolfrey
Grayling and How to Catch Them – F. M. Walbran
The Rod and Line – H. Wheatley
River Angling for Salmon and Trout – J. Younger
Three in Norway by Two of Them

The Flyfisher's Classic Library – Coch-y-Bonddu Books
Machynlleth, Mid-Wales
01654 702837
www.ffcl.com   www.anglebooks.com